MORE EASY PIANO HYMNS

FOR BEGINNERS

A BOOK OF MUSIC FOR PRAISE AND WORSHIP

COLLECTED AND ARRANGED BY
ANGELA MARSHALL

More Easy Piano Hymns for Beginners

A Book of Music for Praise and Worship

ISBN: 978-1-960555-25-0

Published by Avanell Publishing Inc

www.avanellpublishing.com

Bonus Downloads

This book includes free digital content.
Visit **www.avanellpublishing.com** or scan the QR code below
to access your bonus materials,

- Fully orchestrated recordings of each song

- Printable reference charts to use while you play

- Lessons and charts for left hand playing

- Practice tips to help you build your skills

- Sheet music of additional songs

Table of Contents

How to Read Piano Music..............................6

Level One 8

    I Shall Not Be Moved........................10

    O Happy Day................................12

    Jesus, Lover of My Soul....................14

    Lord, I Hear of Showers of Blessings 16

    I Surrender All............................18

    Christ the Lord is Risen Today.............20

    Grace Greater than Our Sin 22

    Nothing but the Blood of Jesus 24

Level Two 26

    I'm So Glad Jesus Lifted Me 28

    Amazing Love (And Can It Be?)..............30

    What a Mighty God We Serve 32

    Depth of Mercy 34

    Steal Away.................................36

    We Have an Anchor..........................38

    My God is So Great.........................40

    Sinners, Turn 42

    Lead Me to Calvary 44

    Power in the Blood 46

Level Three 48

    For He Alone is Worthy.....................50

    Send Me, Jesus 52

    The Way of the Cross Leads Home 54

    Jesus Saves 56

    Where He Leads Me 58

Table of Contents

Level Four 60

I Love to Tell the Story 62

I've Got the Joy, Joy, Joy 64

Must Jesus Bear the Cross Alone? 66

Hallelujah! What a Savior! 68

Saved, Saved! 70

Pass Me Not, Oh Gentle Savior 72

What a Friend We Have in Jesus 74

Glory to His Name 76

Level Five 78

The B-I-B-L-E 80

A Charge to Keep I Have 81

Jesus Loves the Little Children 82

Count Your Blessings 84

Just As I Am 86

Wade in the Water 88

Love Divine, All Loves Excelling 90

Sweet Hour of Prayer 92

Rejoice, the Lord is King 94

Soldiers of Christ, Arise 96

It Is Well 98

Blessed Assurance 100

The Old Rugged Cross 102

How to Read Piano Music

A B C D E F G

Piano keys are named after the letters of the alphabet, but they only go to G!

The piano has black and white keys.
The black keys are arranged in groups of 2 and 3.

The letters **C D E**
are by a group of 2.

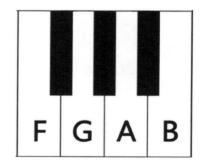

The letters **F G A B**
are by a group of 3.

The pattern of 2 and 3 repeats across the keyboard.
Use the groups of black keys to find the right notes on the piano.

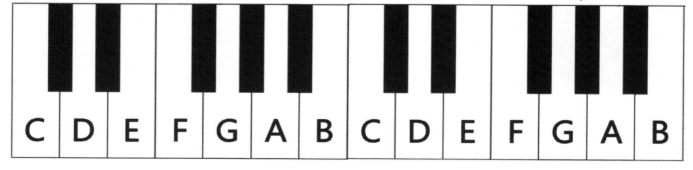

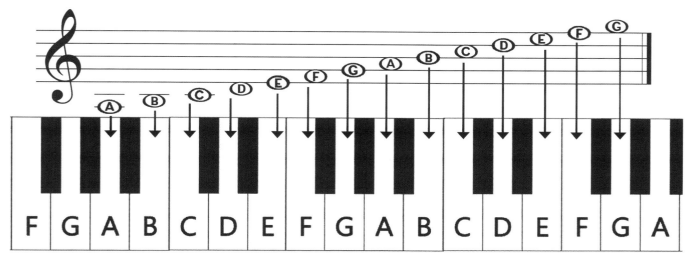

Each note is a letter of the musical alphabet and a key on the piano.

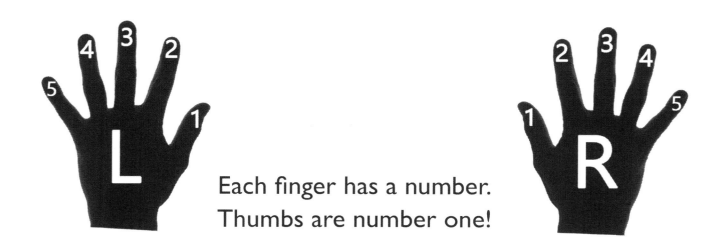

Each finger has a number.
Thumbs are number one!

Each type of note gets a different number of beats.

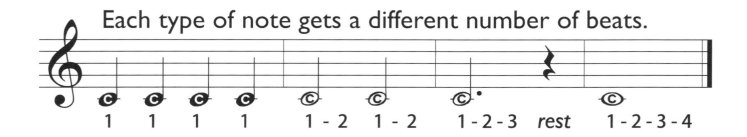

1　　1　　1　　1　　　1 - 2　　1 - 2　　1 - 2 - 3　*rest*　　1 - 2 - 3 - 4

Level One

I Shall Not Be Moved 10

O Happy Day 12

Jesus, Lover of My Soul 14

Lord, I Hear of Showers of Blessings 16

I Surrender All 18

Christ the Lord is Risen Today 20

Grace Greater than Our Sin 22

Nothing but the Blood of Jesus 24

The songs in Level One only use five notes.

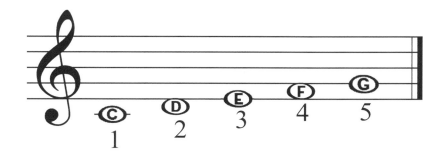

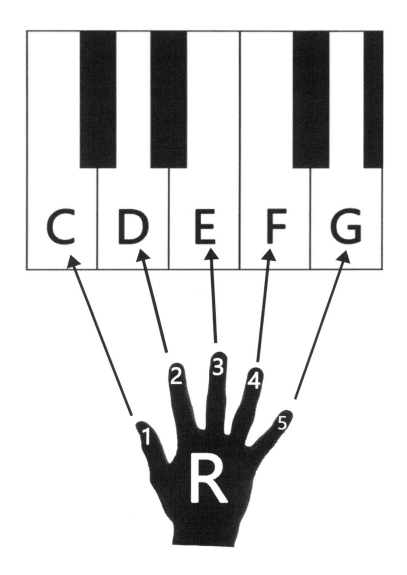

I Shall Not Be Moved

African American Spiritual

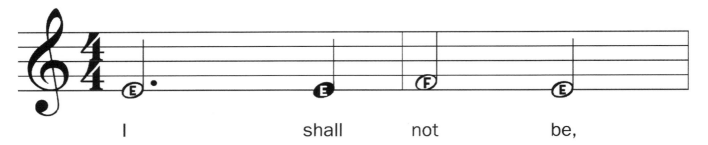

I　　　　shall　　　not　　　be,

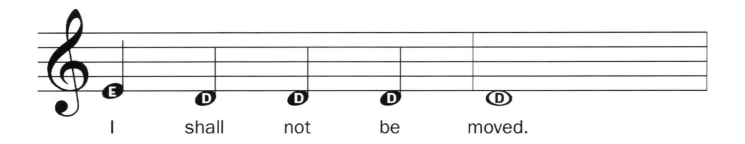

I　　shall　　not　　be　　moved.

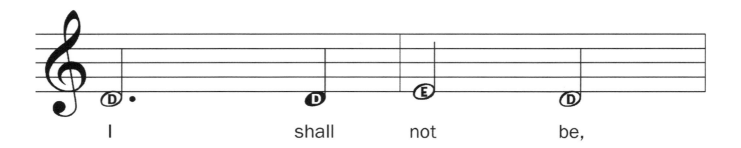

I　　　　shall　　　not　　　be,

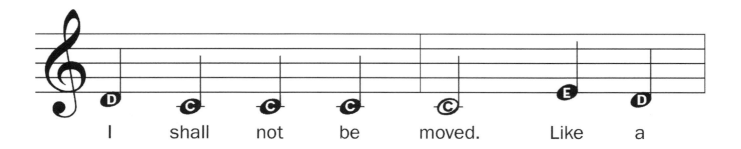

I　shall　not　be　moved.　Like　a

I Shall Not Be Moved

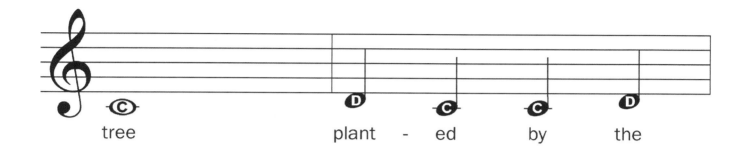

tree   plant - ed   by   the

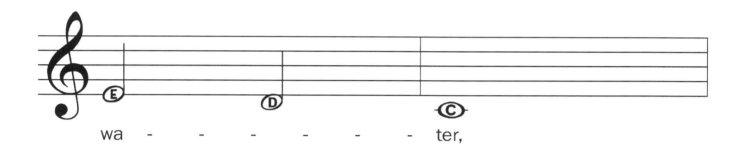

wa - - - - - - ter,

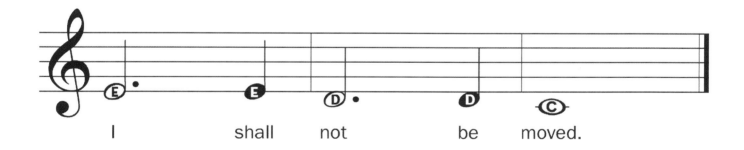

I   shall   not   be   moved.

O Happy Day

Philip Doddridge and William McDonald

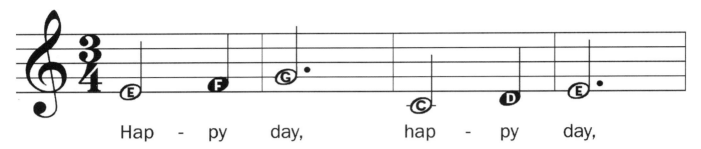

Hap - py day, hap - py day,

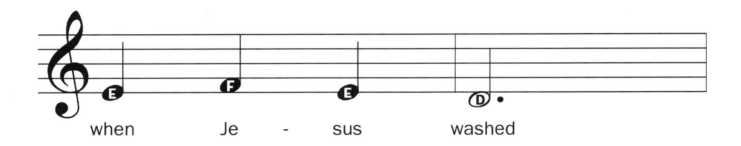

when Je - sus washed

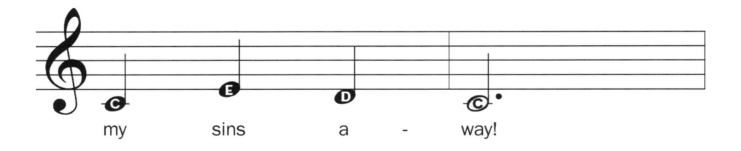

my sins a - way!

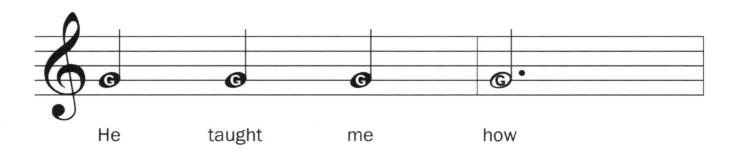

He taught me how

O Happy Day

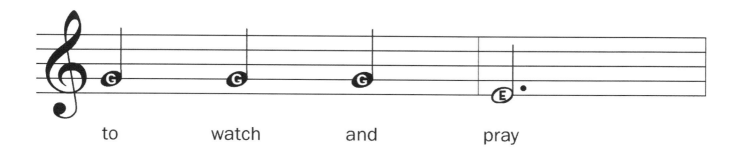

to   watch   and   pray

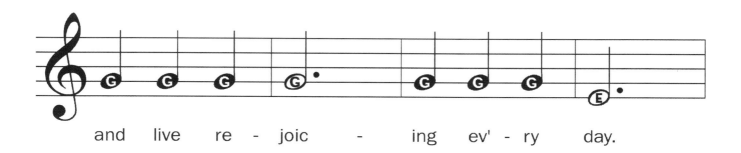

and   live   re - joic   -   ing   ev' - ry   day.

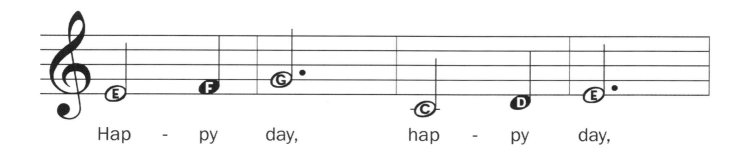

Hap - py   day,   hap - py   day,

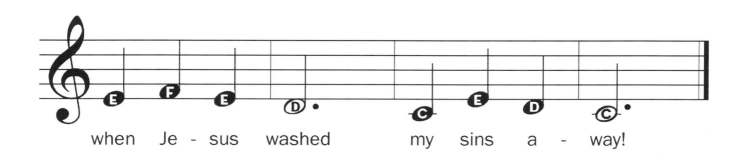

when   Je - sus   washed   my   sins   a - way!

Jesus, Lover of My Soul

Charles Wesley and Simeon B. Marsh

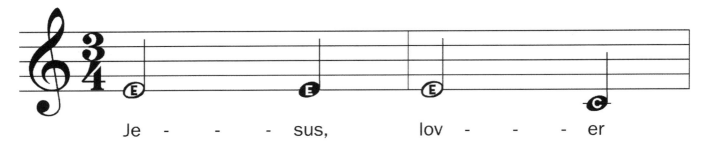

Je - - - sus,   lov - - - er

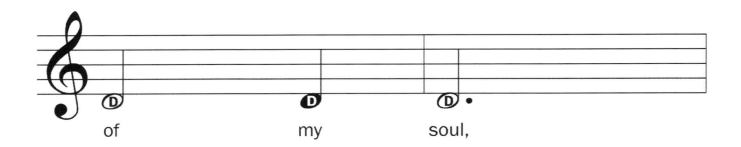

of   my   soul,

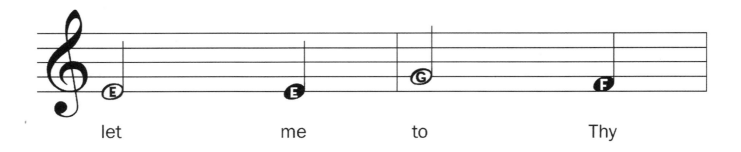

let   me   to   Thy

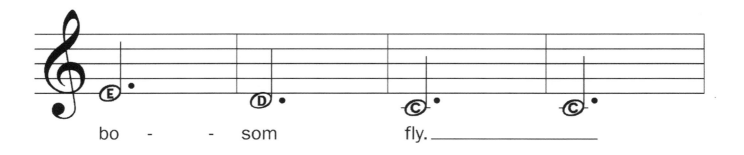

bo - - som   fly. _____

Jesus, Lover of My Soul

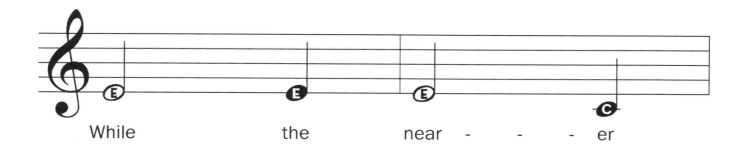

While   the   near -   -   -   er

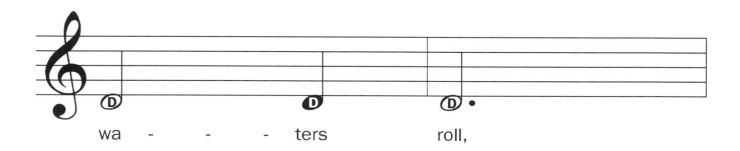

wa -   -   -   ters   roll,

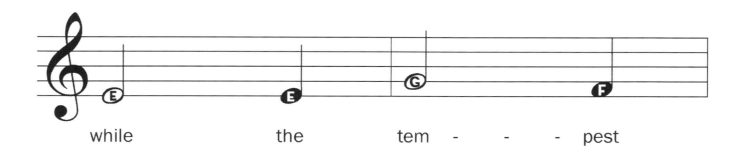

while   the   tem -   -   -   pest

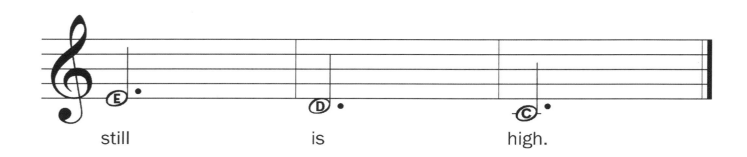

still   is   high.

Lord, I Hear of Showers of Blessings

Elizabeth Codner and William B. Bradbury

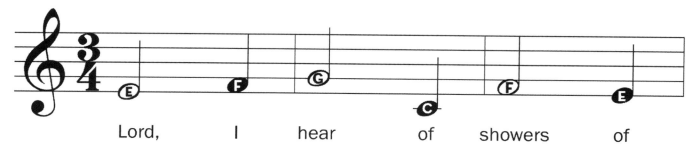

Lord,   I   hear   of   showers   of

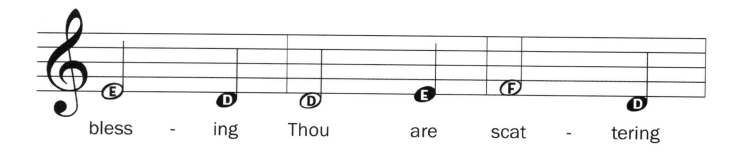

bless - ing   Thou   are   scat - tering

full   and   free.   Showers   the

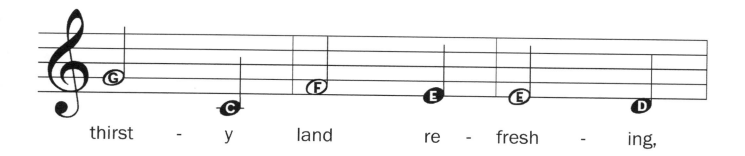

thirst - y   land   re - fresh - ing,

Lord, I Hear of Showers of Blessings

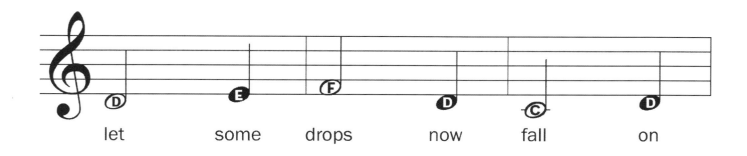

let some drops now fall on

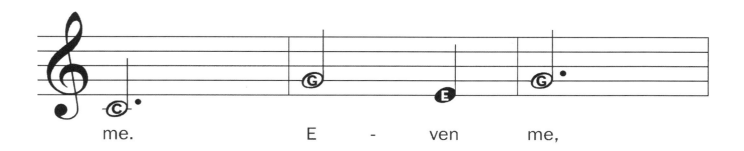

me. E - ven me,

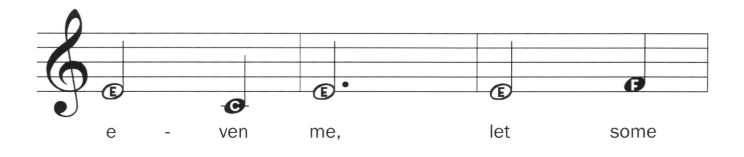

e - ven me, let some

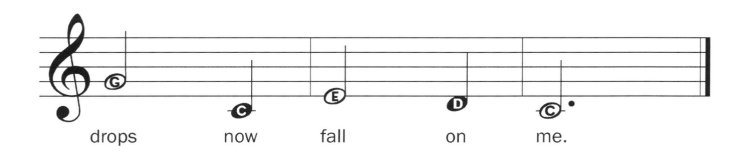

drops now fall on me.

I Surrender All

Judson W. Van De Venter

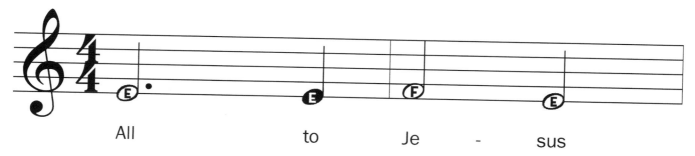

All   to   Je -   sus

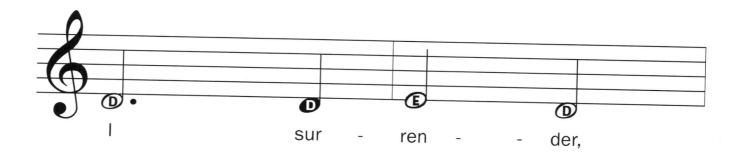

I   sur - ren - - der,

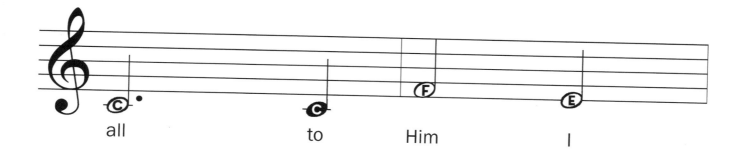

all   to   Him   I

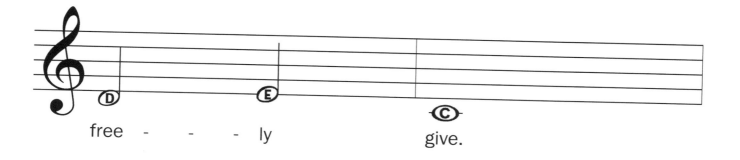

free - - - ly   give.

I Surrender All

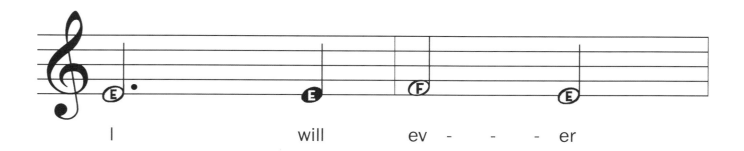

I   will   ev - - - er

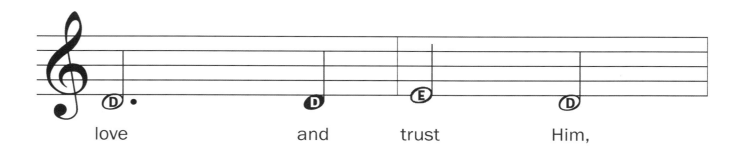

love   and   trust   Him,

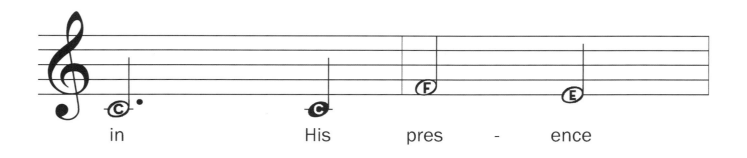

in   His   pres - ence

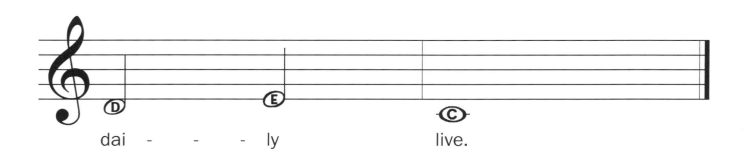

dai - - - ly   live.

Christ the Lord is Risen Today

Wipo of Burgundy, Jane E. Leeson, and Robert Williams

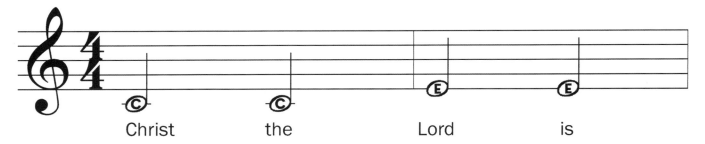

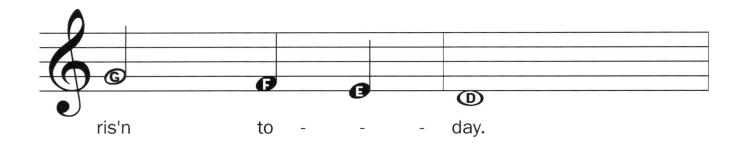

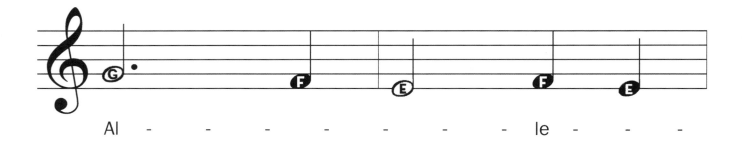

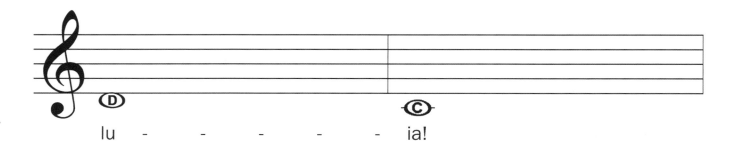

Christ the Lord is Risen Today

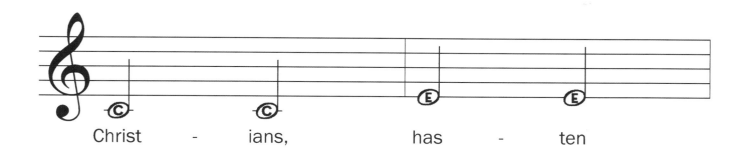

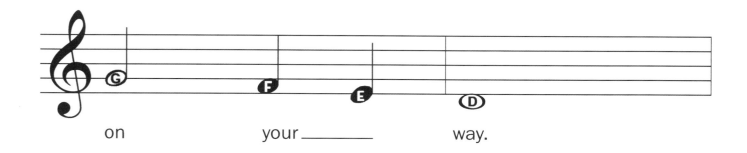

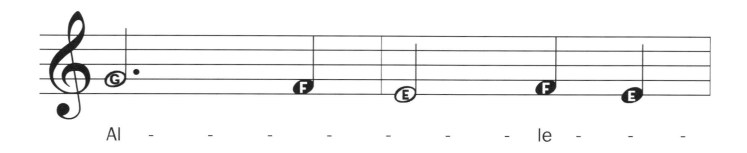

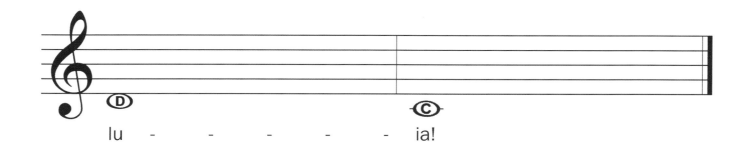

Grace Greater than Our Sin

Julia H. Johnston and Daniel B. Towner

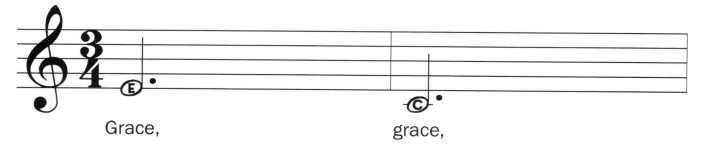

Grace,   grace,

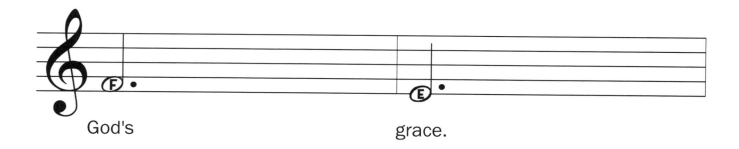

God's   grace.

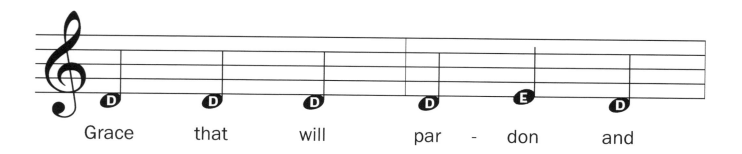

Grace   that   will   par - don   and

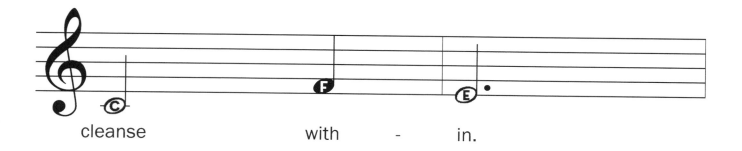

cleanse   with -   in.

Grace Greater than Our Sin

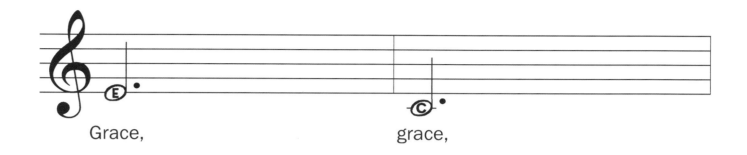

Grace,   grace,

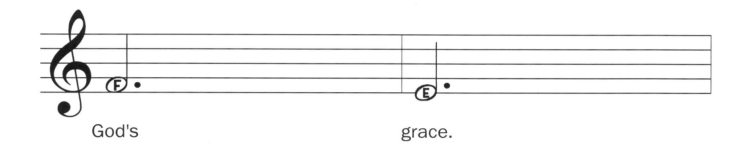

God's   grace.

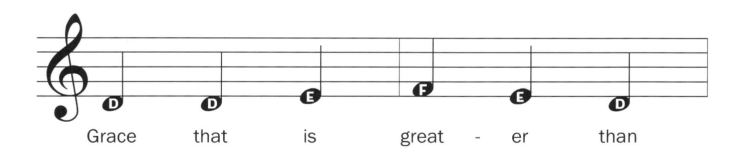

Grace   that   is   great - er   than

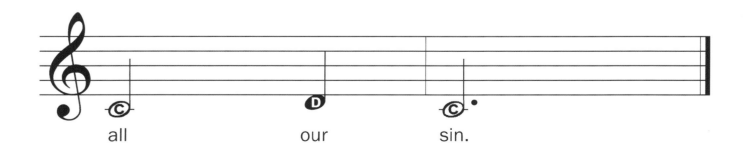

all   our   sin.

Nothing but the Blood of Jesus

Robert Lowry

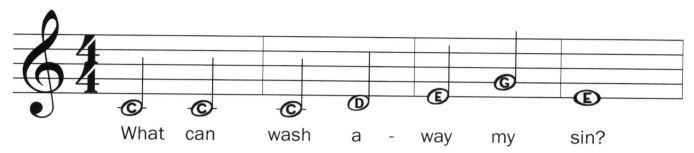

What can wash a - way my sin?

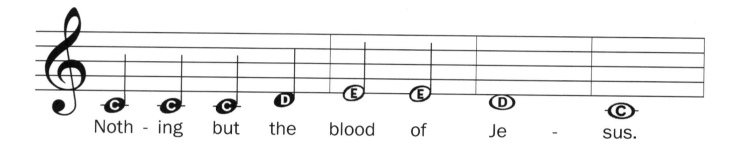

Noth - ing but the blood of Je - sus.

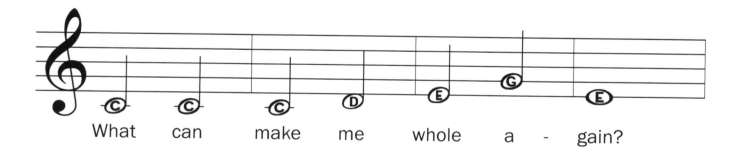

What can make me whole a - gain?

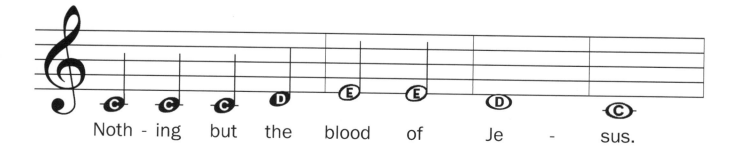

Noth - ing but the blood of Je - sus.

Nothing but the Blood of Jesus

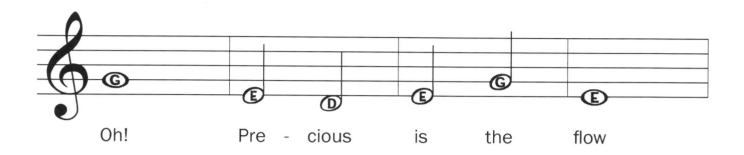

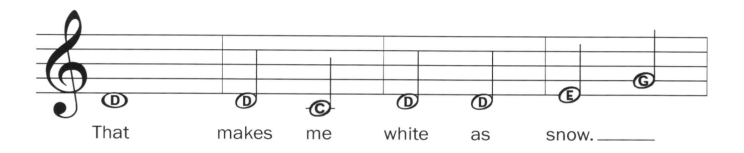

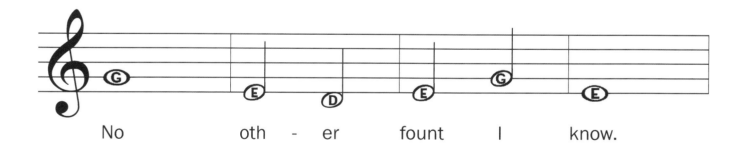

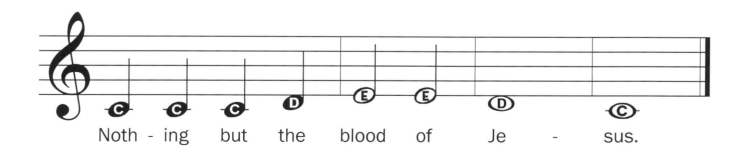

Level Two

I'm So Glad Jesus Lifted Me 28

Amazing Love (And Can It Be?).....................30

What a Mighty God We Serve 32

Depth of Mercy 34

Steal Away..36

We Have an Anchor.......................................38

My God is So Great 40

Sinners, Turn 42

Lead Me to Calvary 44

Power in the Blood 46

The songs in Level Two add two notes.

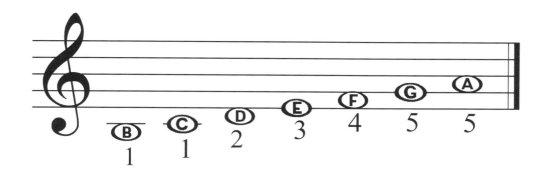

Move fingers one and five to the side to reach the new notes.

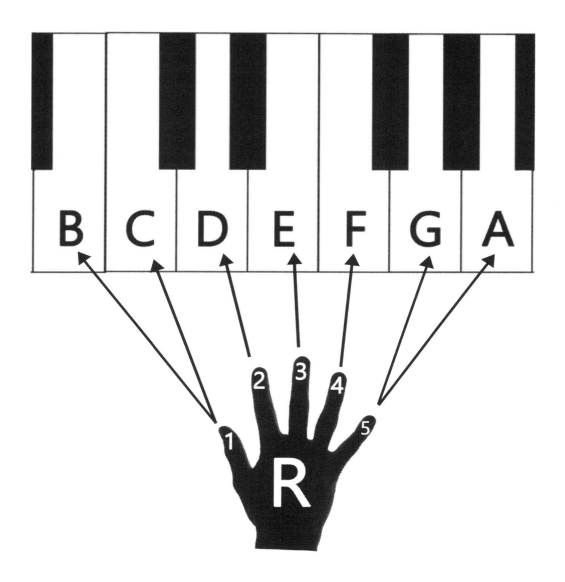

I'm So Glad Jesus Lifted Me

African American Spiritual

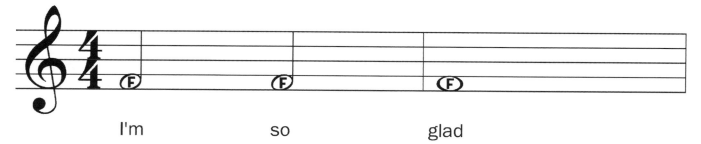

I'm   so   glad

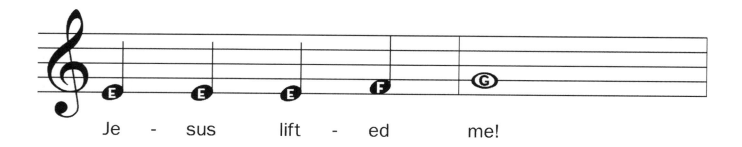

Je - sus   lift - ed   me!

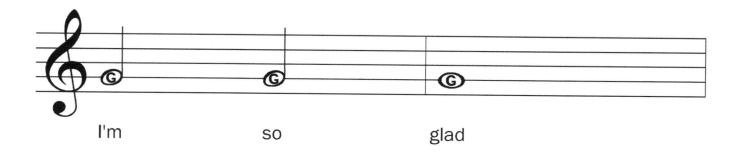

I'm   so   glad

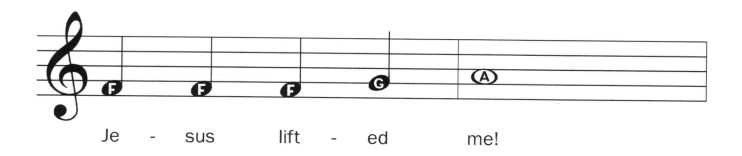

Je - sus   lift - ed   me!

I'm So Glad Jesus Lifted Me

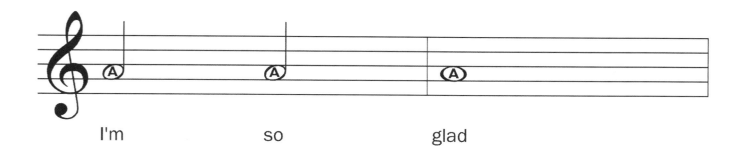

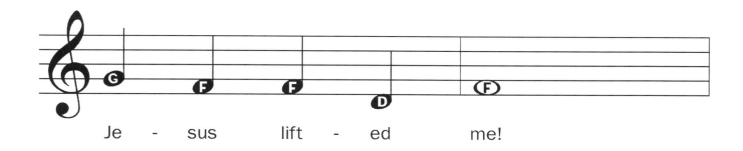

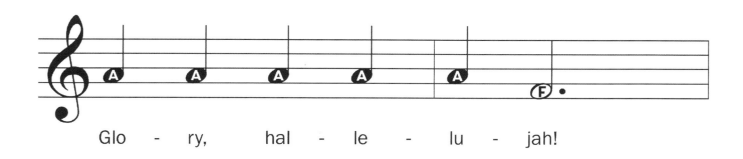

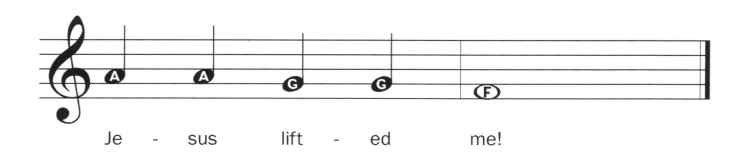

Amazing Love (And Can It Be?)

Charles Wesley and Thomas Campbell

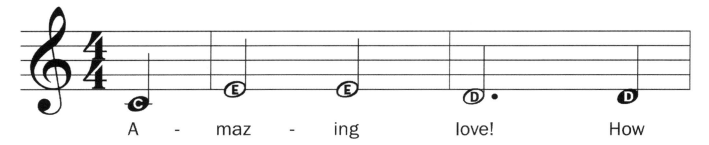

A - maz - ing love! How

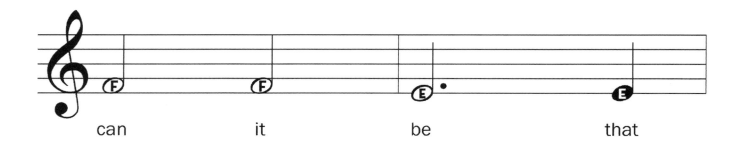

can it be that

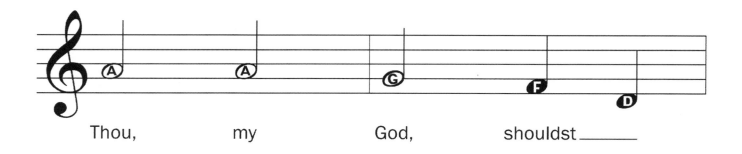

Thou, my God, shouldst _____

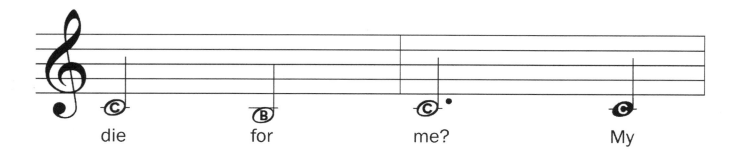

die for me? My

Amazing Love (And Can It Be?)

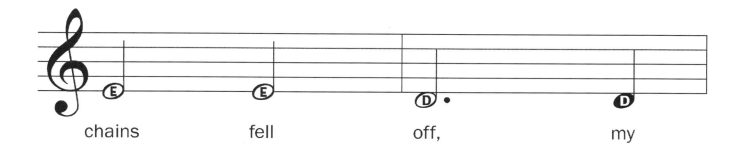

chains   fell   off,   my

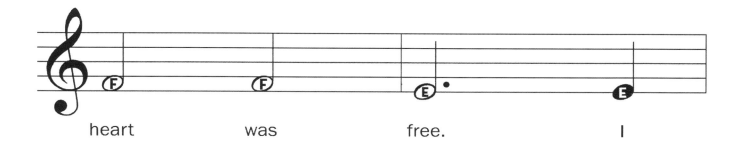

heart   was   free.   I

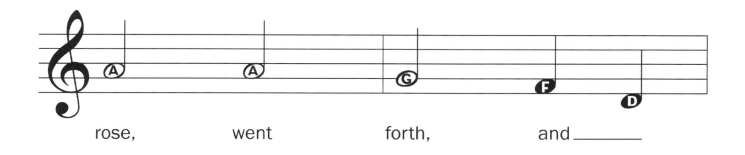

rose,   went   forth,   and_____

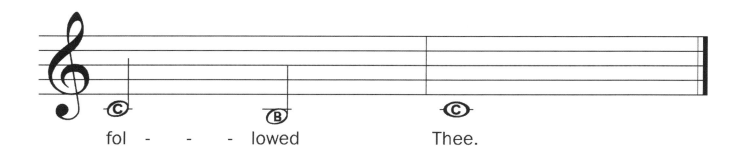

fol - - - lowed   Thee.

What a Mighty God We Serve

Traditional

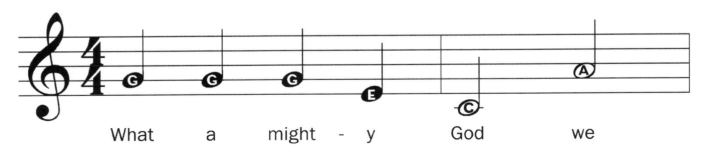

What a might - y God we

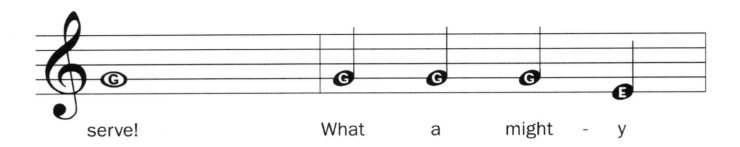

serve! What a might - y

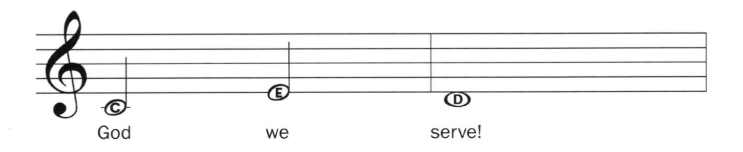

God we serve!

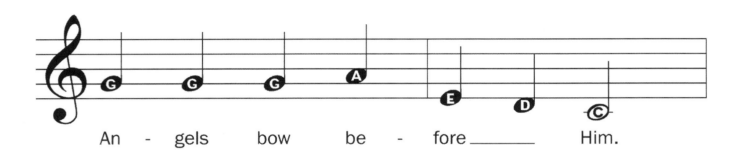

An - gels bow be - fore Him.

What a Mighty God We Serve

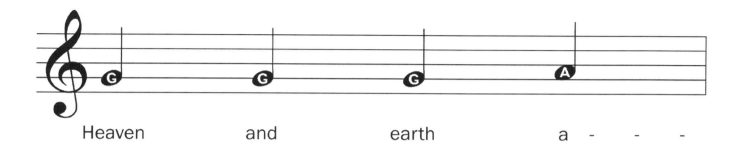

Heaven　　　and　　　earth　　　a - - -

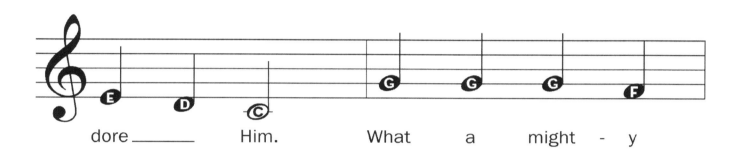

dore_____　Him.　　What　　a　　might - y

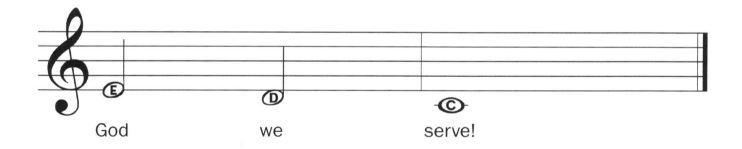

God　　　we　　　serve!

Depth of Mercy

Charles Wesley and Carl M. von Weber

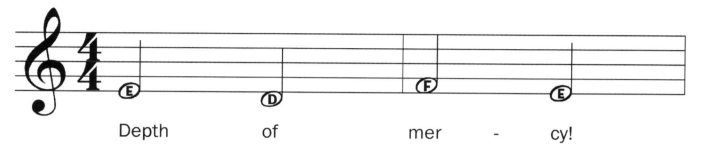

Depth   of   mer -   cy!

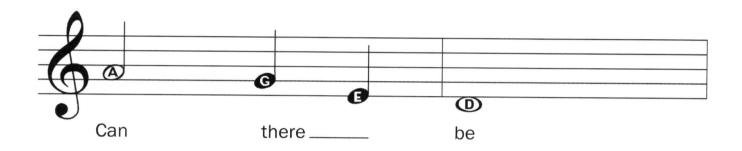

Can   there   be

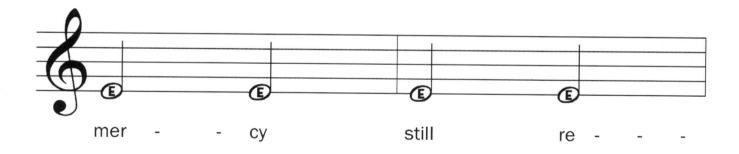

mer - -   cy   still   re - - -

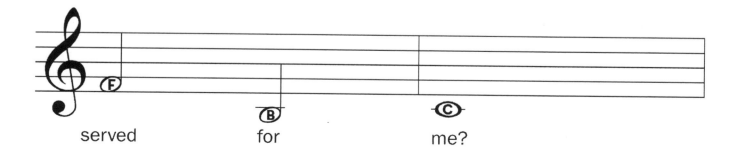

served   for   me?

Depth of Mercy

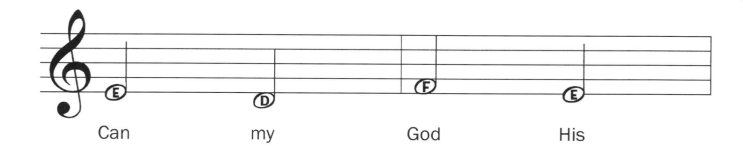

Can my God His

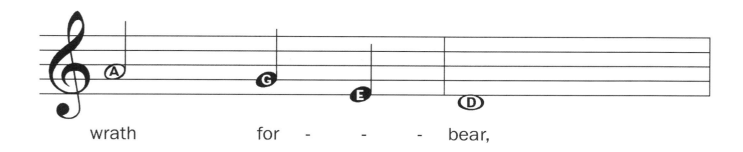

wrath for - - - bear,

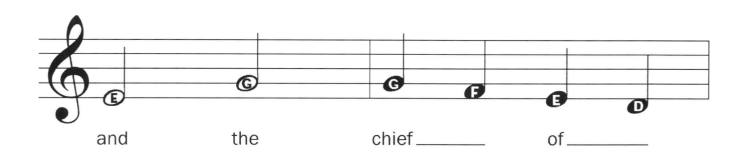

and the chief _____ of _____

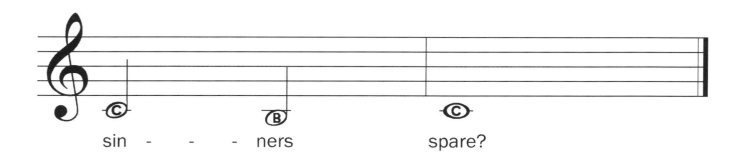

sin - - - ners spare?

Steal Away

African American Spiritual

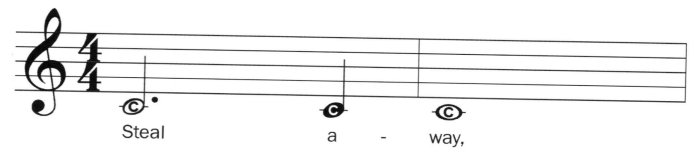

Steal   a - way,

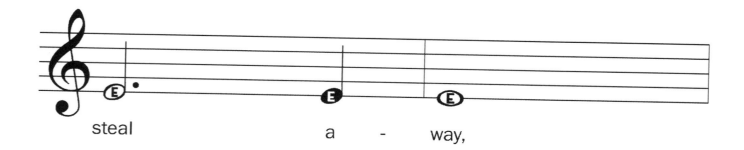

steal   a - way,

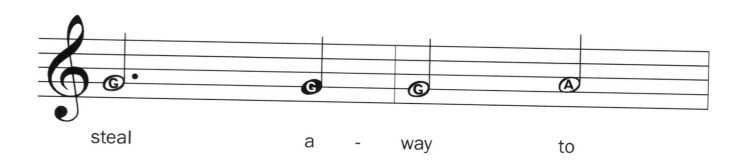

steal   a - way   to

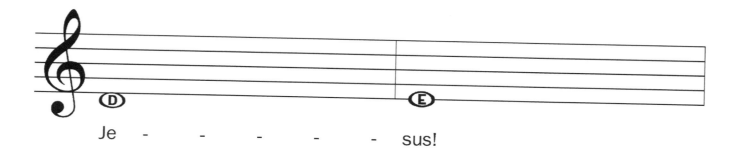

Je - - - - - - sus!

Steal Away

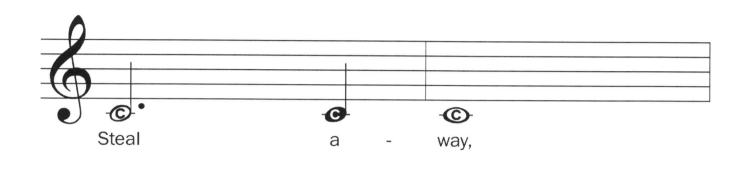

Steal   a - way,

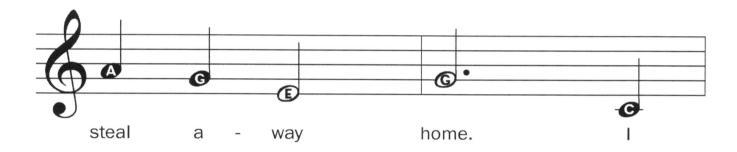

steal   a - way   home.   I

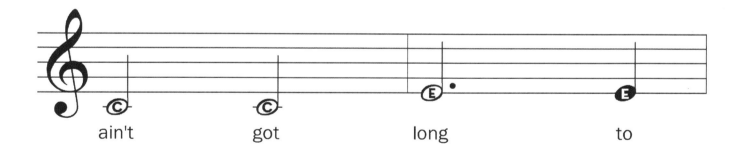

ain't   got   long   to

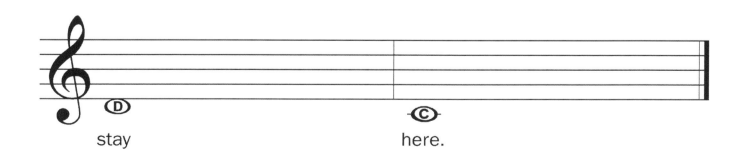

stay   here.

We Have an Anchor

Priscilla J. Owens and William J. Kirkpatrick

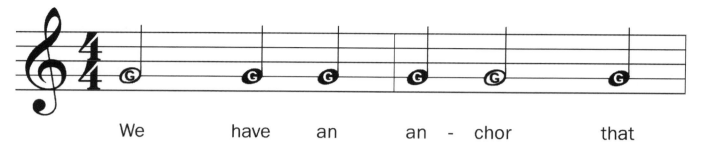

We   have   an   an - chor   that

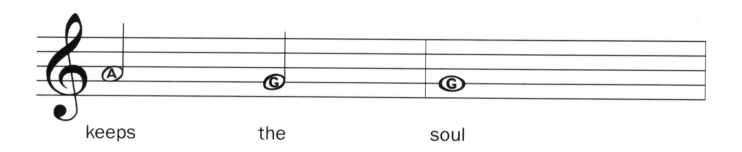

keeps   the   soul

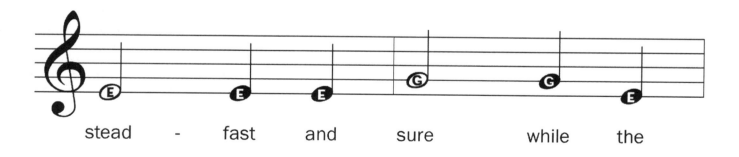

stead - fast and sure while the

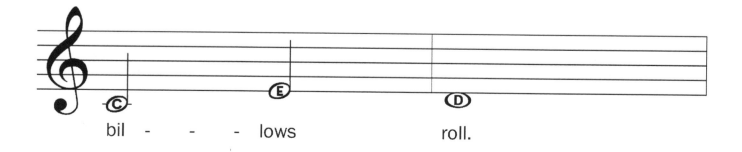

bil - - - lows   roll.

We Have an Anchor

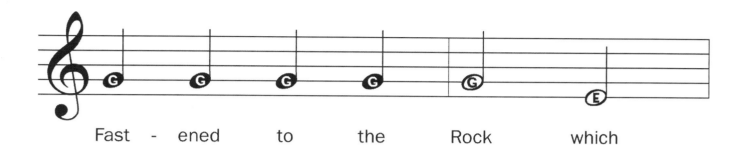

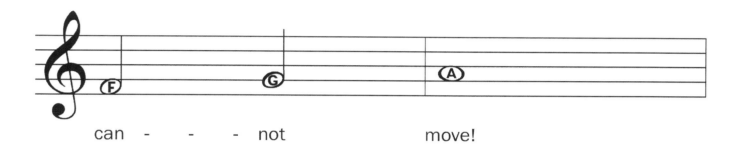

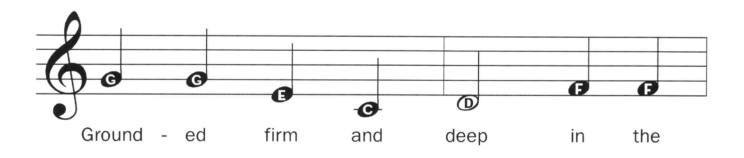

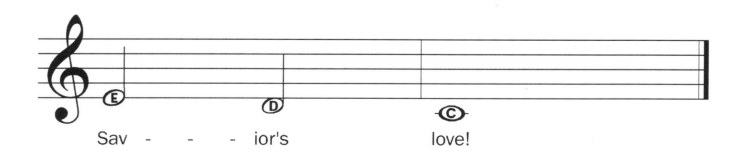

My God is So Great

Traditional Children's Folk Song

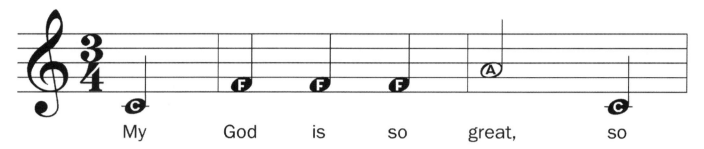

My   God   is   so   great,   so

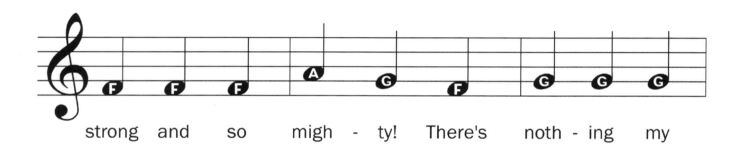

strong   and   so   migh - ty!   There's   noth - ing   my

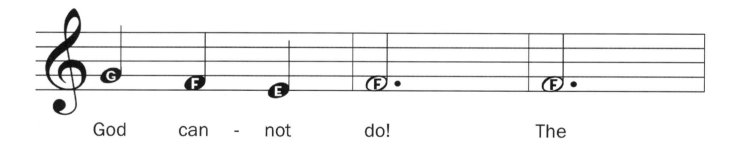

God   can - not   do!   The

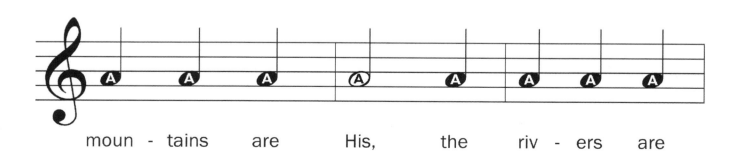

moun - tains   are   His,   the   riv - ers   are

My God is So Great

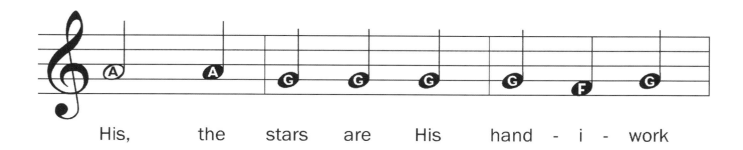

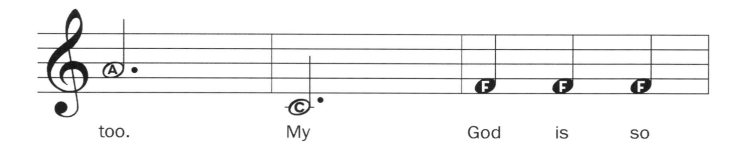

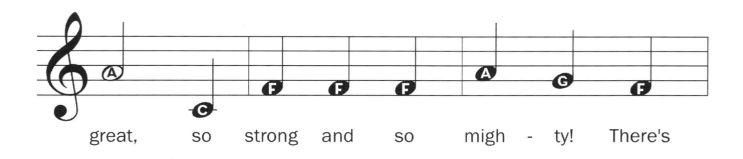

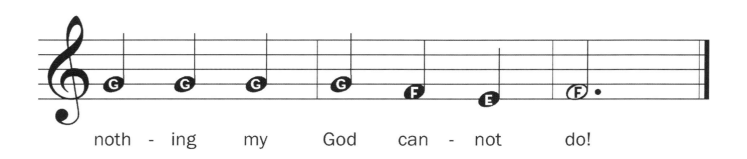

Sinners, Turn

Charles Wesley and Ferdinand Hérold

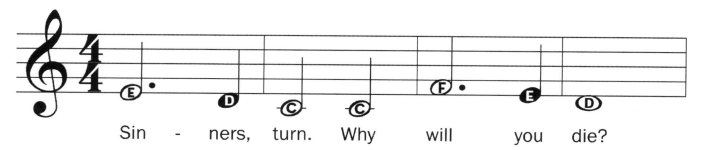

Sin - ners, turn. Why will you die?

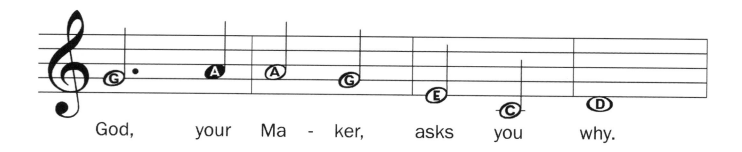

God, your Ma - ker, asks you why.

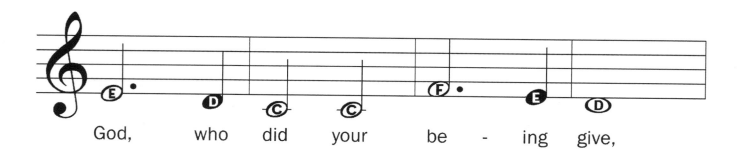

God, who did your be - ing give,

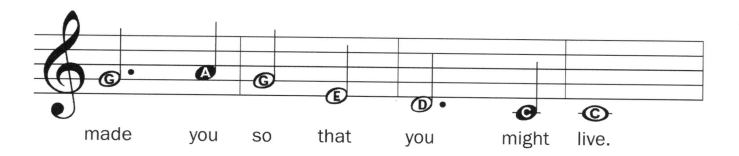

made you so that you might live.

Sinners, Turn

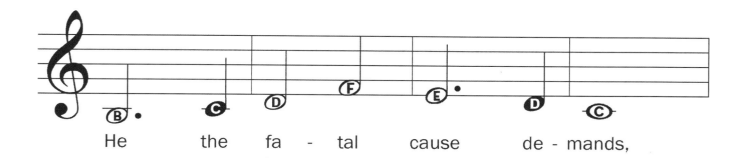

He   the   fa - tal   cause   de - mands,

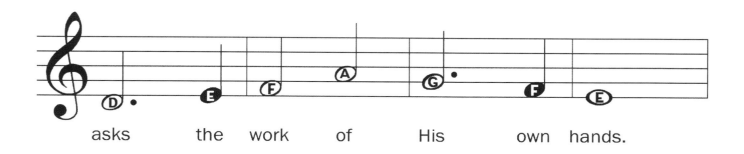

asks   the   work   of   His   own   hands.

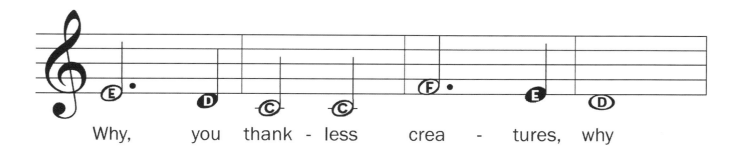

Why,   you   thank - less   crea - tures,   why

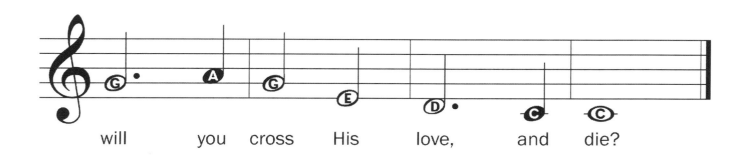

will   you   cross   His   love,   and   die?

Lead Me to Calvary

Jennie Evelyn Hussey and William J. Kirkpatrick

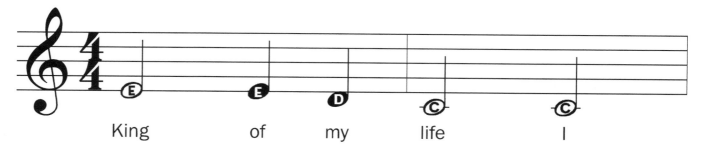

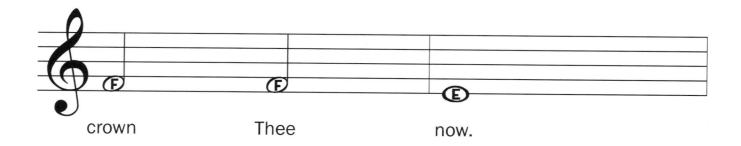

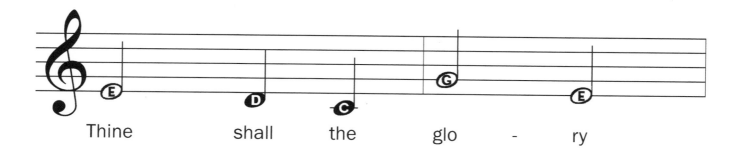

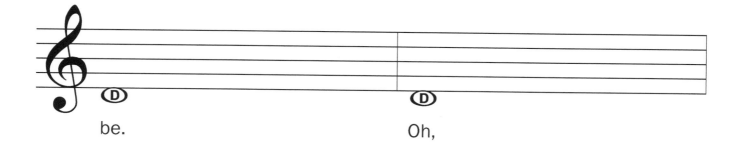

Lead Me to Calvary

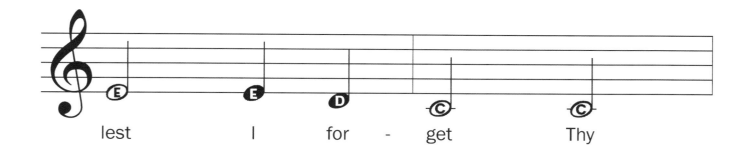

lest   I   for - get   Thy

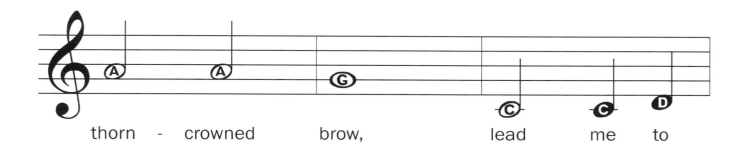

thorn - crowned   brow,   lead   me   to

Cal - - va - - ry.

Power in the Blood

Lewis E. Jones

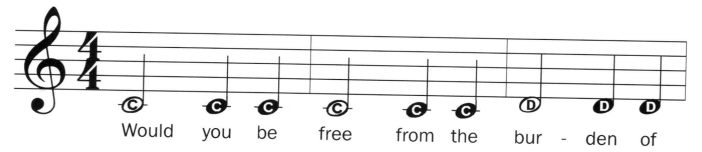

Would you be free from the bur - den of

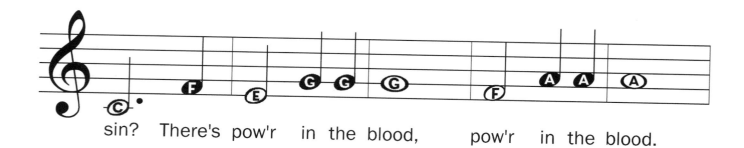

sin? There's pow'r in the blood, pow'r in the blood.

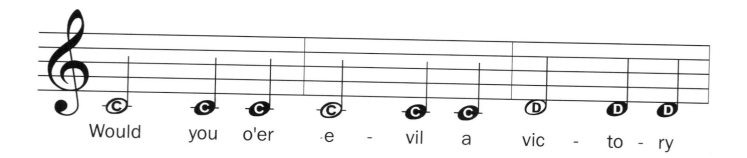

Would you o'er -e - vil a vic - to - ry

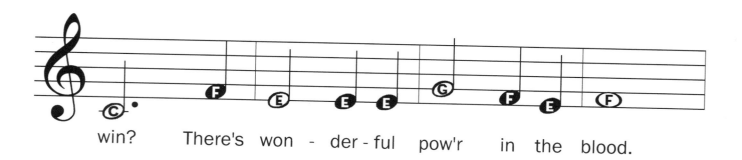

win? There's won - der - ful pow'r in the blood.

Power in the Blood

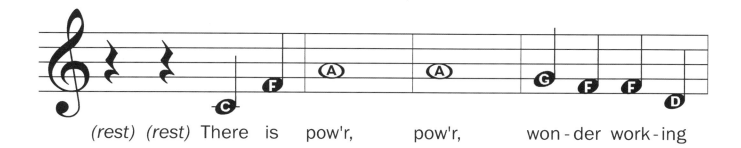

(rest) (rest) There is pow'r, pow'r, won-der work-ing

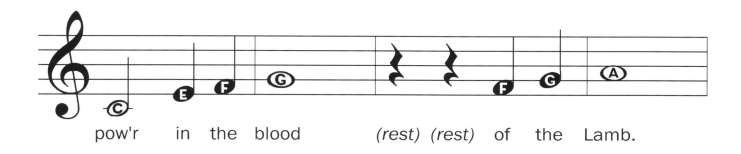

pow'r in the blood (rest) (rest) of the Lamb.

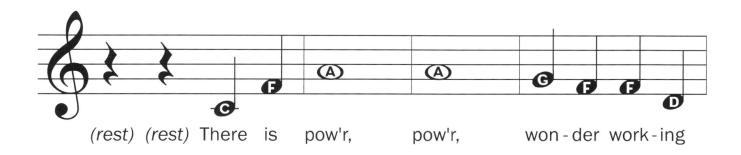

(rest) (rest) There is pow'r, pow'r, won-der work-ing

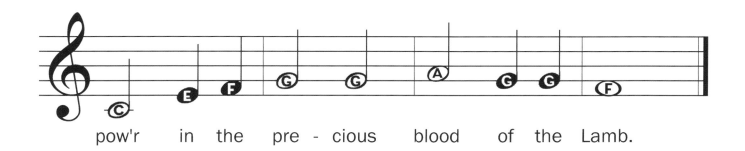

pow'r in the pre - cious blood of the Lamb.

Level Three

For He Alone is Worthy.................................. 50

Send Me, Jesus.. 52

The Way of the Cross Leads Home 54

Jesus Saves 56

Where He Leads Me 58

The songs in Level Three use both hands.

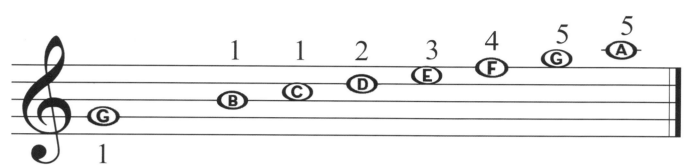

The left hand only plays one note.

The right hand plays the same notes, but sits higher to make room for the left hand.

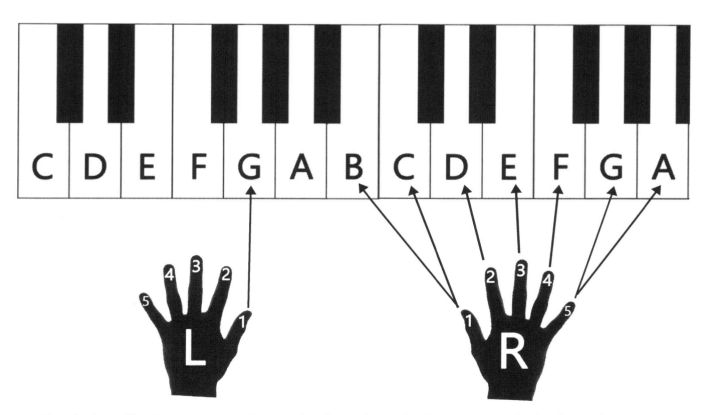

Find the G closest to the right hand and place your left thumb on it.

For He Alone is Worthy

Traditional

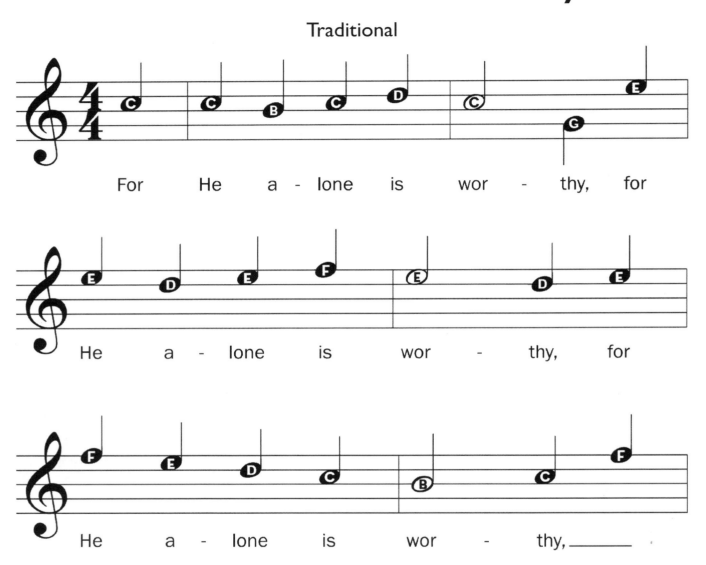

For He a - lone is wor - thy, for

He a - lone is wor - thy, for

He a - lone is wor - thy, _____

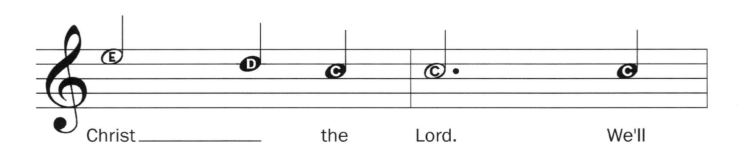

Christ _____ the Lord. We'll

For He Alone is Worthy

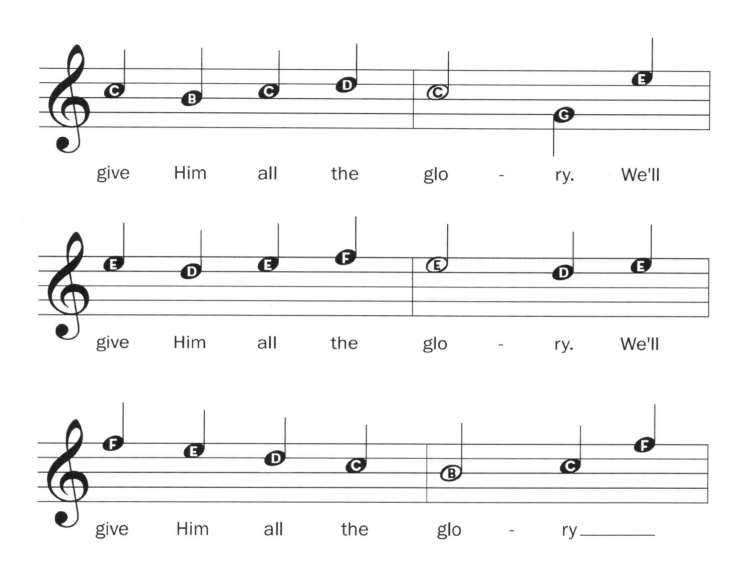

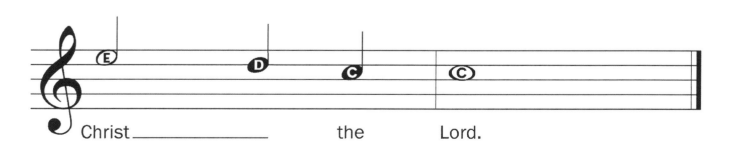

Send Me, Jesus

Traditional South African Song

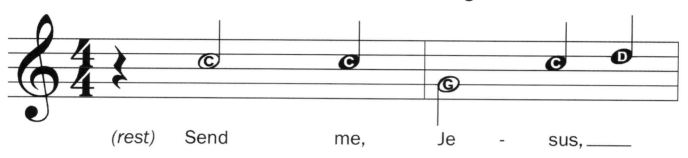

(rest)   Send   me,   Je - sus, _____

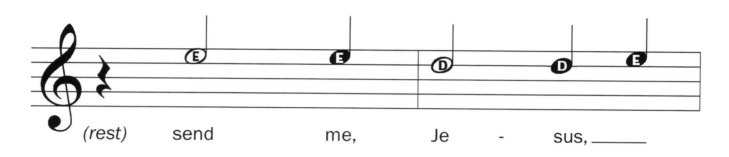

(rest)   send   me,   Je - sus, _____

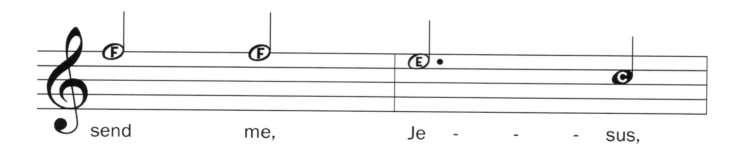

send   me,   Je - - - sus,

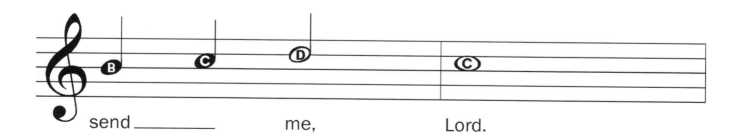

send _____ me,   Lord.

Send Me, Jesus

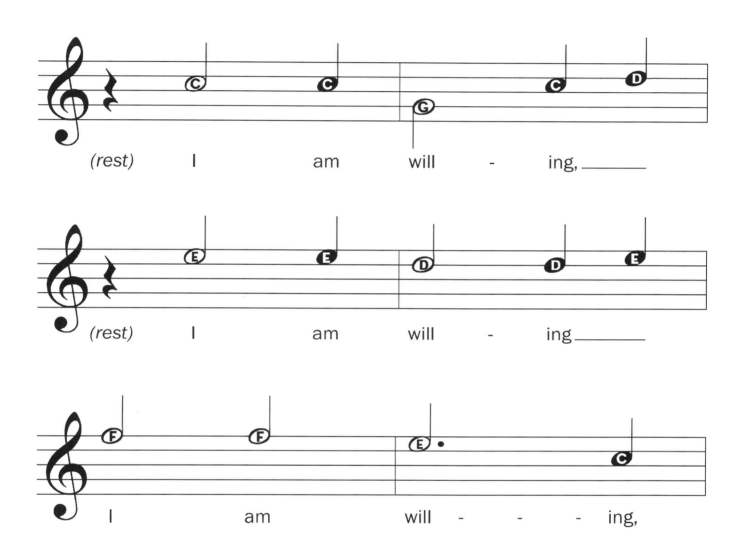

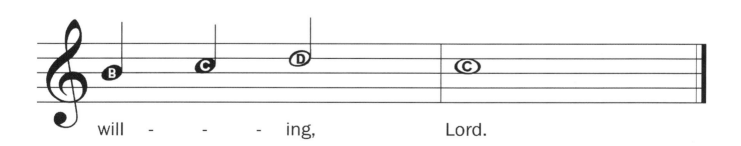

The Way of the Cross Leads Home

Jessie B. Pounds and Charles H. Gabriel

The Way of the Cross Leads Home

Jesus Saves

Priscilla J. Owens and William J. Kirkpatrick

Jesus Saves

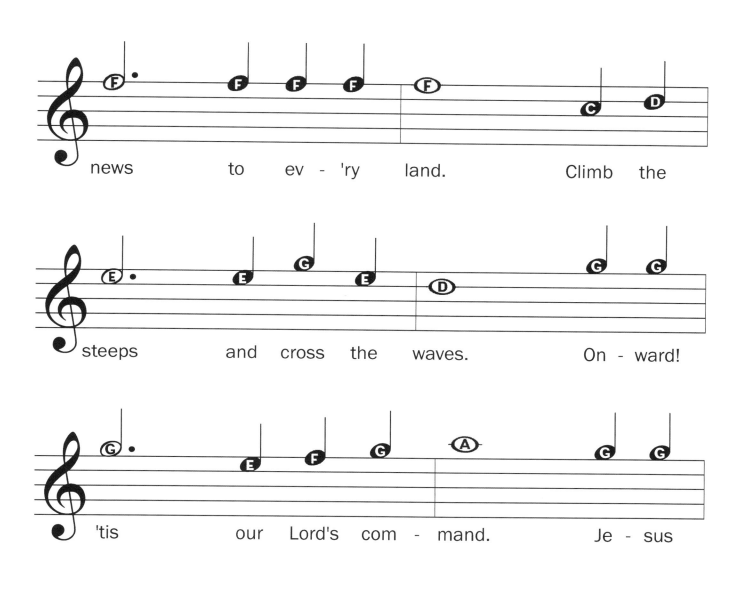

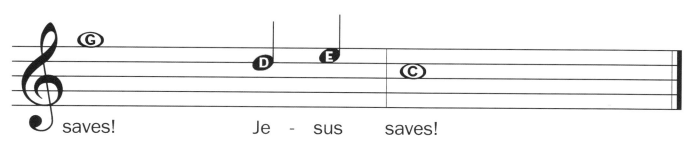

Where He Leads Me

E.W. Blandly and J.S. Norris

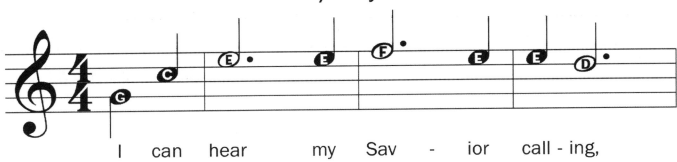

I can hear my Sav - ior call - ing,

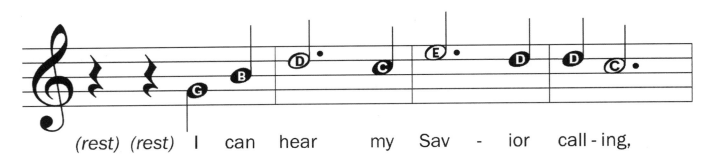

(rest) (rest) I can hear my Sav - ior call - ing,

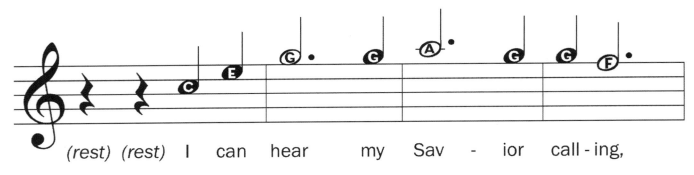

(rest) (rest) I can hear my Sav - ior call - ing,

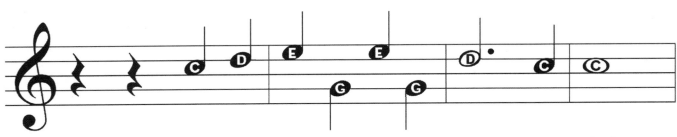

(rest) (rest) "Take thy cross and fol - low, fol - low Me."

Where He Leads Me

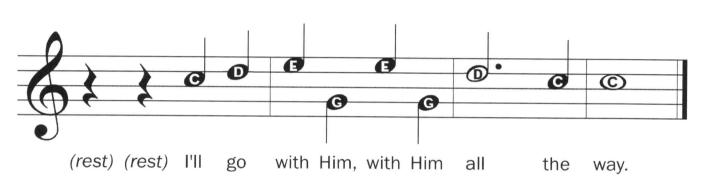

Level Four

I Love to Tell the Story 62

I've Got the Joy, Joy, Joy 64

Must Jesus Bear the Cross Alone? 66

Hallelujah! What a Savior! 68

Saved, Saved! 70

Pass Me Not, Oh Gentle Savior 72

What a Friend We Have in Jesus 74

Glory to His Name 76

The songs in Level Four use three left hand notes.

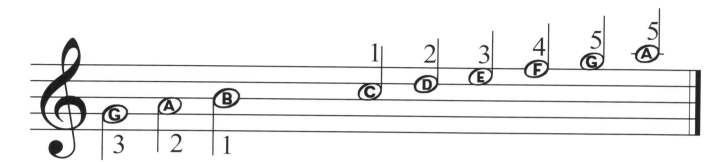

The left hand plays notes
with the stem pointing down.

The right hand plays notes
with the stem pointing up.

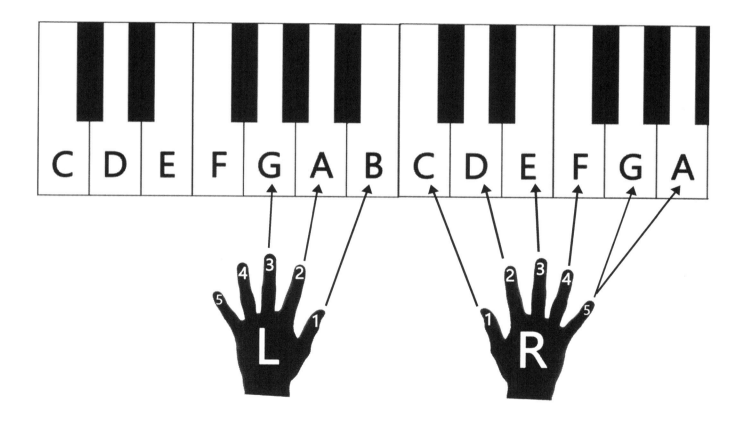

Your thumbs will sit beside each other on the keyboard.

For notes without a stem, use the notes around them as a guide,
or check this chart to see which hand should play the note.

I Love to Tell the Story

Kate Hankey and William G. Fischer

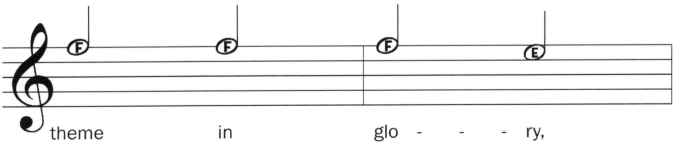

I Love to Tell the Story

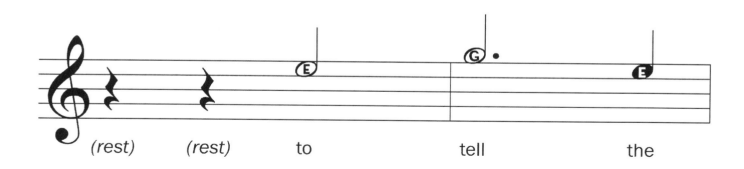

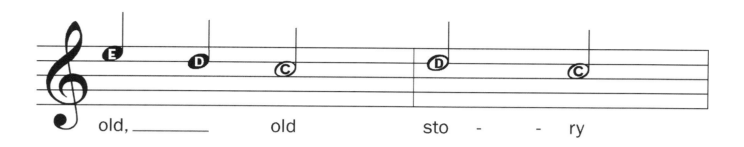

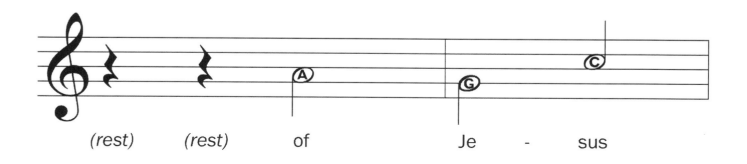

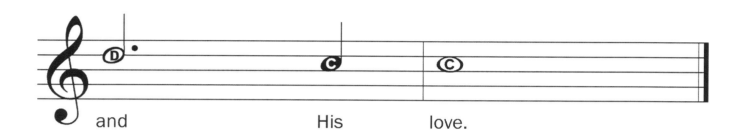

I've Got the Joy, Joy, Joy

George W. Cooke

I've Got the Joy, Joy, Joy

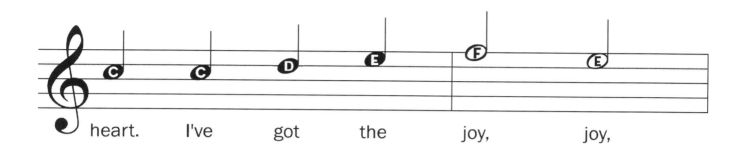

heart.   I've   got   the   joy,   joy,

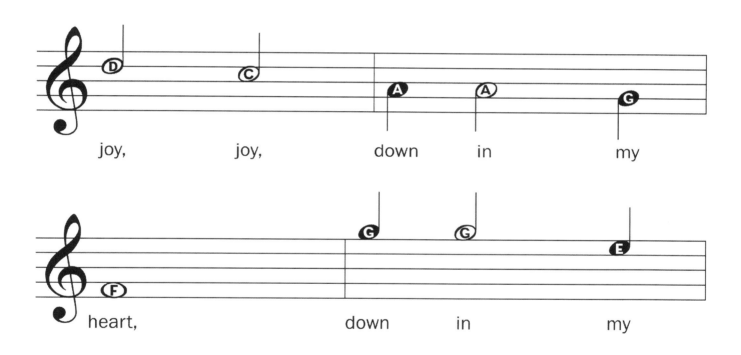

joy,   joy,   down   in   my

heart,   down   in   my

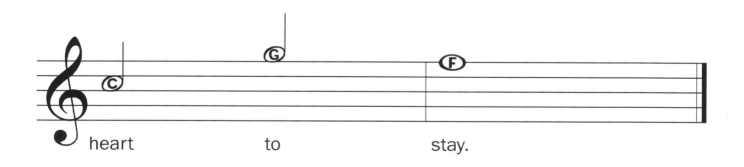

heart   to   stay.

Must Jesus Bear the Cross Alone?

Thomas Shepherd and George N. Allen

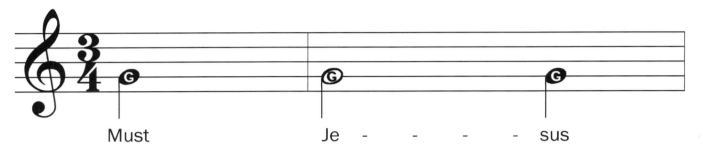

Must   Je - - - - sus

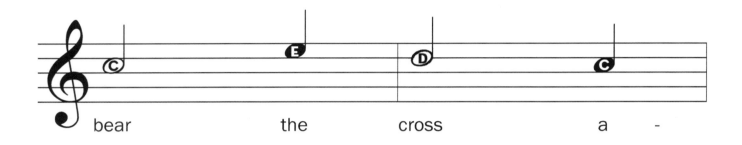

bear   the   cross   a -

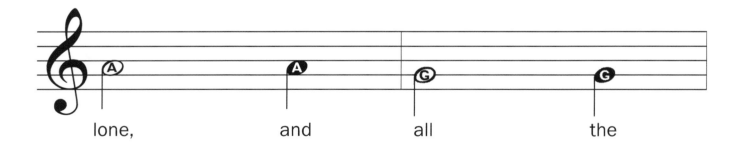

lone,   and   all   the

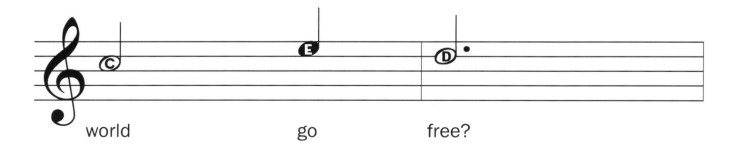

world   go   free?

Must Jesus Bear the Cross Alone?

Hallelujah! What a Savior!

Philip P. Bliss

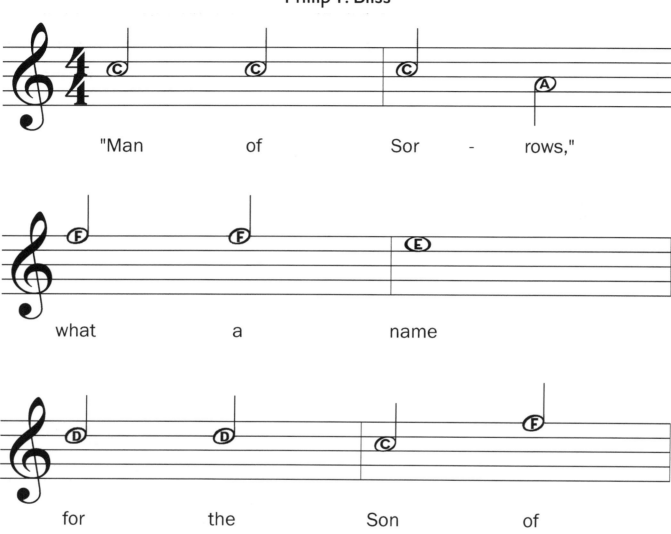

Hallelujah! What a Savior!

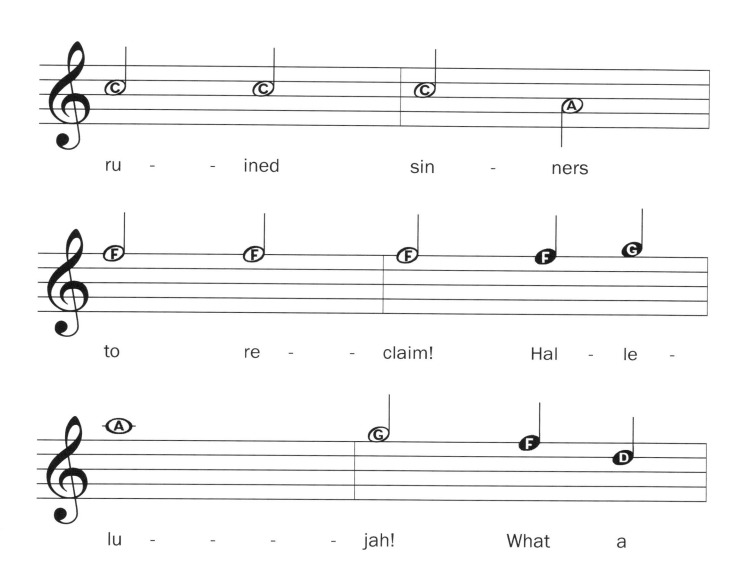

ru - - ined   sin - ners   to   re - - claim!   Hal - le -

lu - - - - jah!   What   a

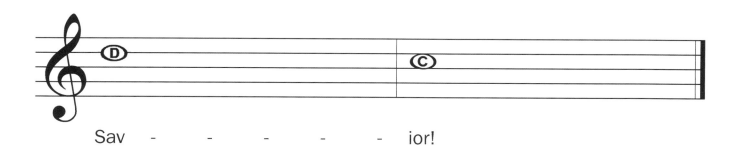

Sav - - - - - ior!

Saved, Saved!

Jack P. Schofield

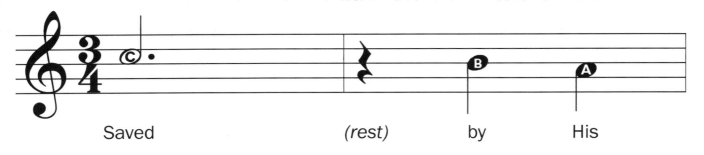

Saved   (rest)   by   His

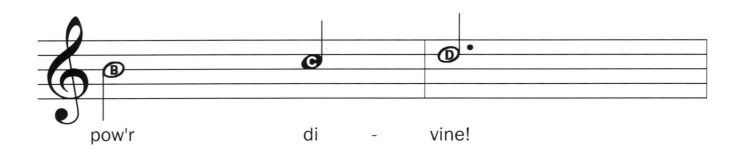

pow'r   di -   vine!

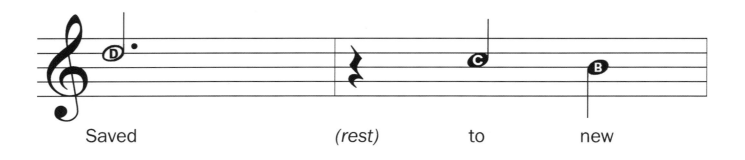

Saved   (rest)   to   new

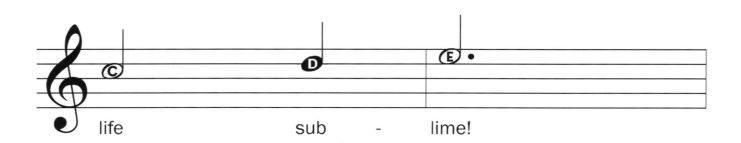

life   sub -   lime!

Saved, Saved!

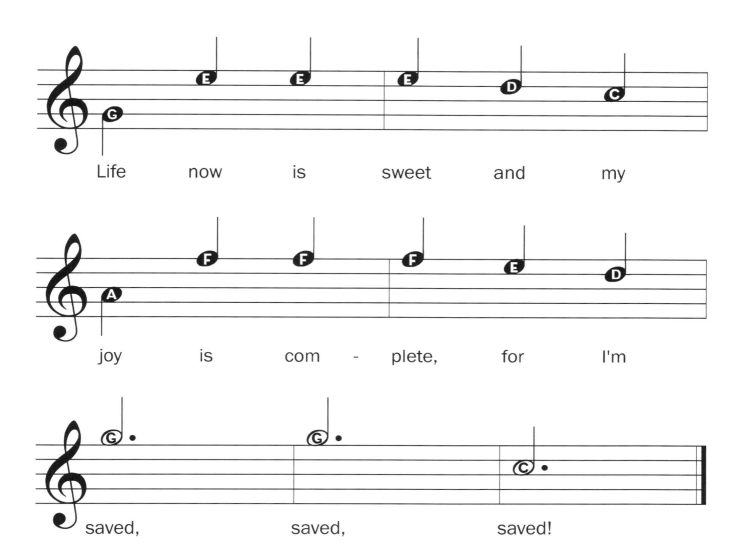

Life   now   is   sweet   and   my

joy   is   com - plete,   for   I'm

saved,   saved,   saved!

Pass Me Not, Oh Gentle Savior

Fanny J. Crosby and William Doane

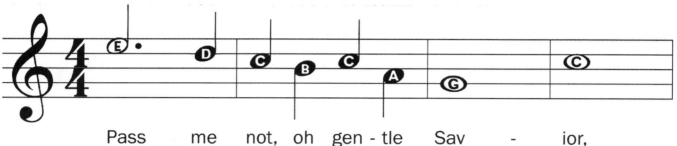

Pass me not, oh gen - tle Sav - ior,

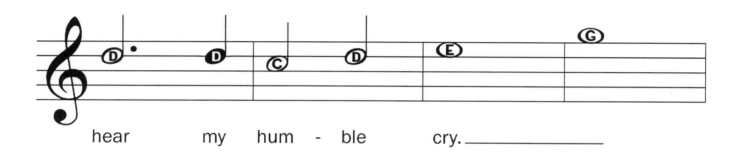

hear my hum - ble cry. _____

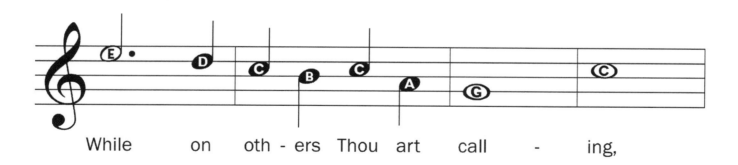

While on oth - ers Thou art call - ing,

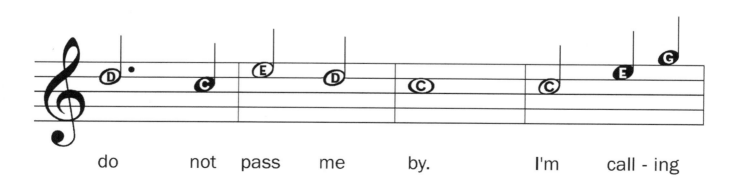

do not pass me by. I'm call - ing

Pass Me Not, Oh Gentle Savior

What a Friend We Have in Jesus

Joseph M. Scriven and Charles C. Converse

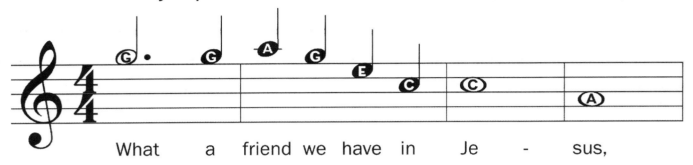

What a friend we have in Je - sus,

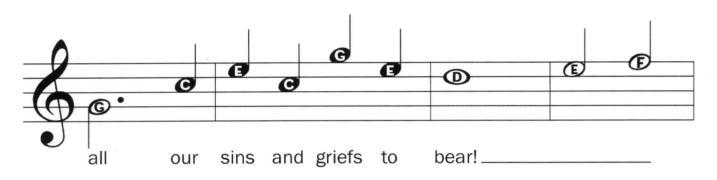

all our sins and griefs to bear!

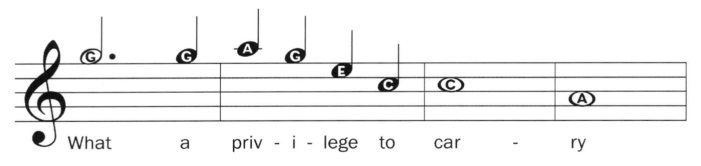

What a priv - i - lege to car - ry

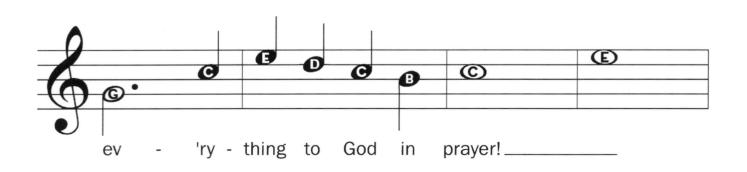

ev - 'ry - thing to God in prayer!

What a Friend We Have in Jesus

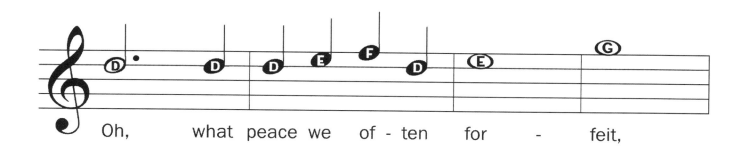

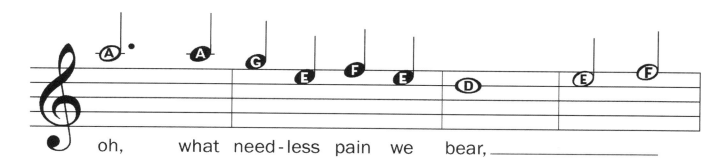

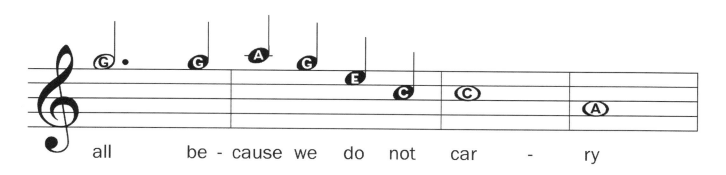

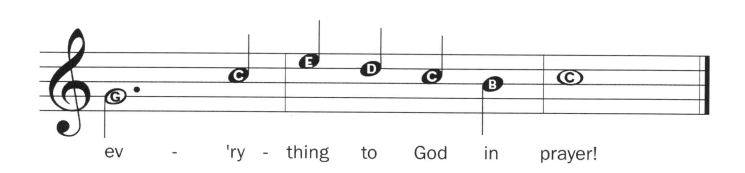

Glory to His Name

E.A. Hoffman and John H. Stockton

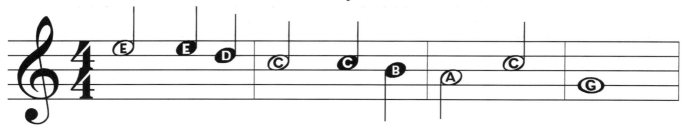

Down at the cross where my Sav - ior died.

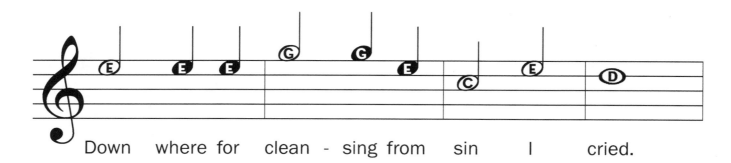

Down where for clean - sing from sin I cried.

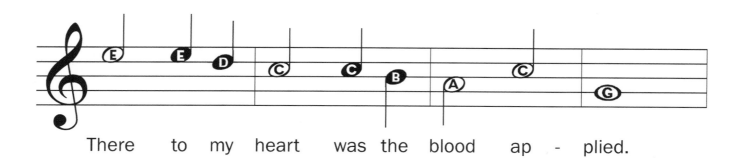

There to my heart was the blood ap - plied.

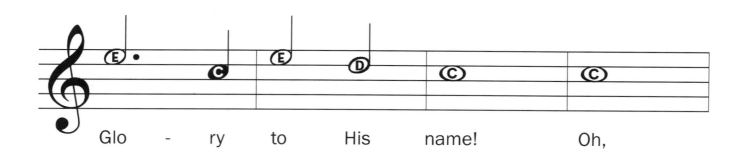

Glo - ry to His name! Oh,

Glory to His Name

Level Five

The B-I-B-L-E 80

A Charge to Keep I Have 81

Jesus Loves the Little Children 82

Count Your Blessings 84

Just As I Am 86

Wade in the Water 88

Love Divine, All Loves Excelling 90

Sweet Hour of Prayer 92

Rejoice, the Lord is King 94

Soldiers of Christ, Arise 96

It Is Well 98

Blessed Assurance 100

The Old Rugged Cross 102

The songs in Level Five use five left hand notes.

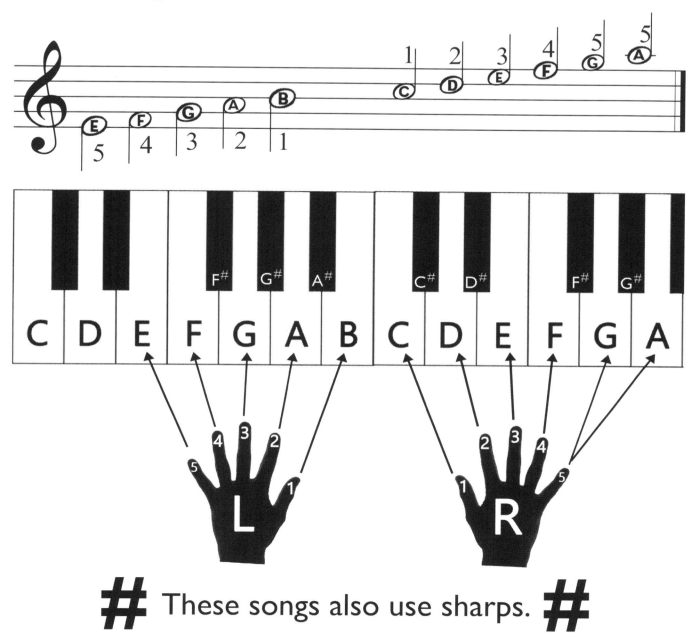

♯ These songs also use sharps. ♯

Sharps tell you to play the black key directly to the right of the written note.

The B-I-B-L-E

Traditional

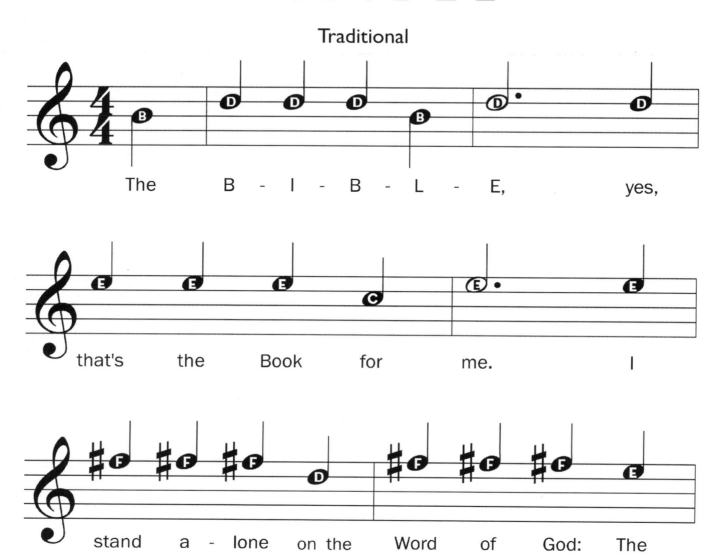

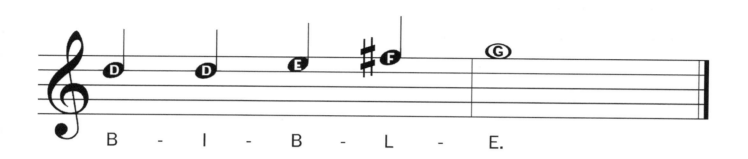

A Charge to Keep I Have

Charles Wesley and Lowell Mason

Jesus Loves the Little Children

C.H. Woolston and George F. Root

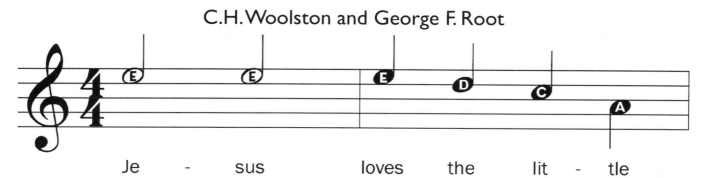

Je - sus   loves   the   lit - tle

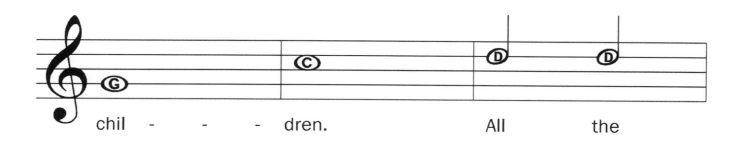

chil - - - dren.   All   the

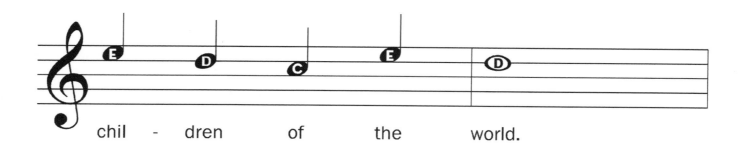

chil - dren   of   the   world.

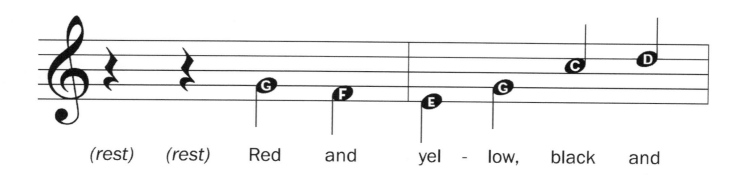

(rest)   (rest)   Red   and   yel - low,   black   and

Jesus Loves the Little Children

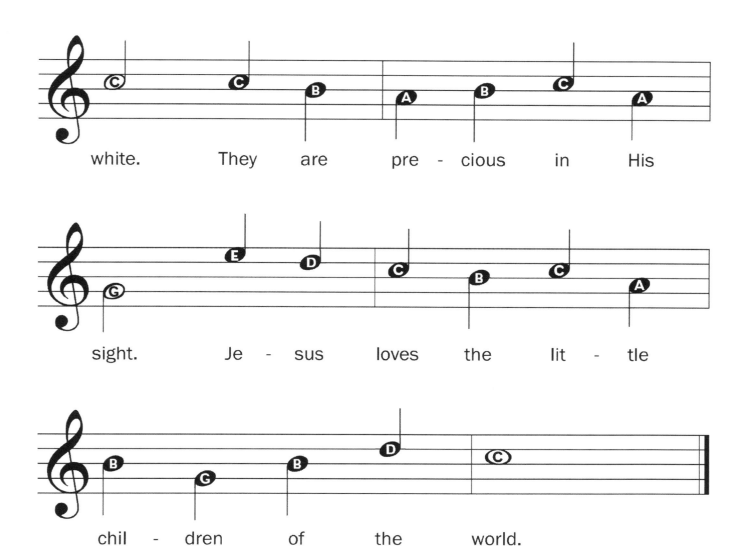

Count Your Blessings

Johnson Oatman Jr. and Edwin O. Excell

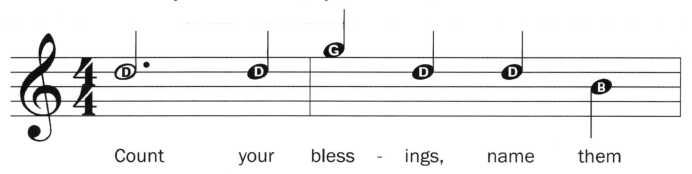

Count your bless - ings, name them

one by one.

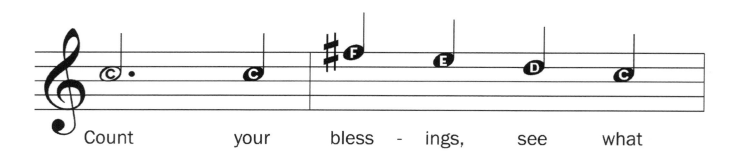

Count your bless - ings, see what

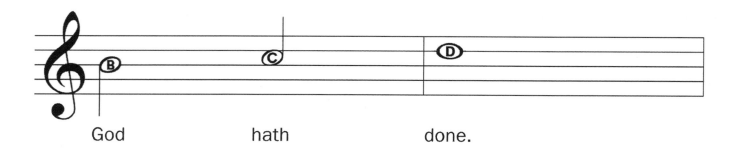

God hath done.

Count Your Blessings

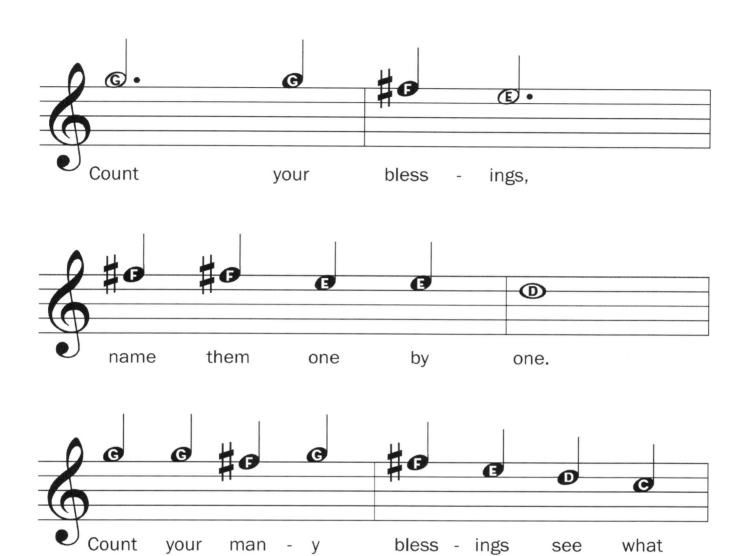

Count your bless - ings,

name them one by one.

Count your man - y bless - ings see what

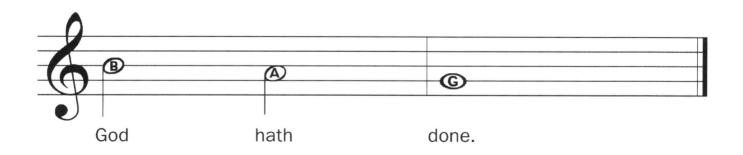

God hath done.

Just As I Am

Charlotte Elliot and William B. Bradbury

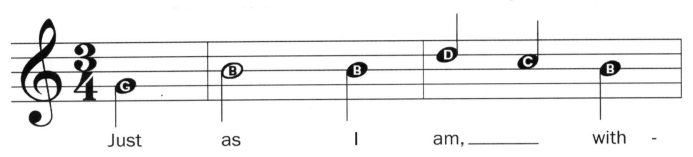

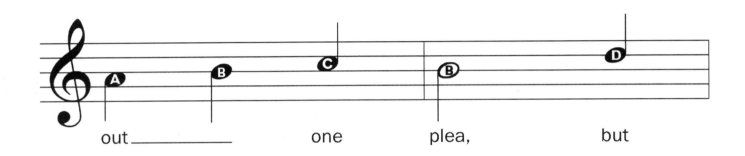

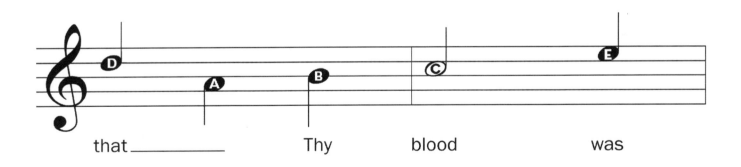

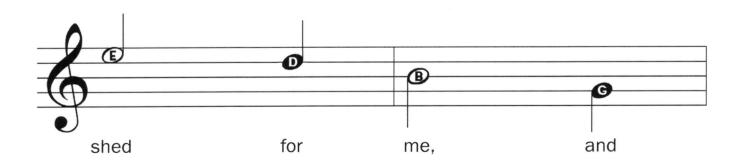

Just As I Am

Wade in the Water

African American Spiritual

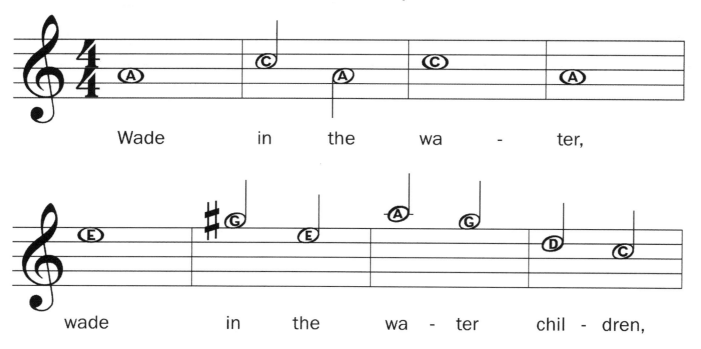

Wade   in   the   wa   -   ter,

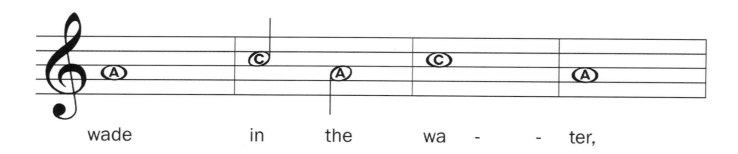

wade   in   the   wa - ter   chil - dren,

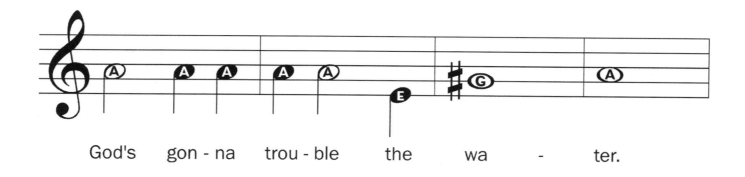

wade   in   the   wa   -   -   ter,

God's   gon - na   trou - ble   the   wa   -   ter.

Wade in the Water

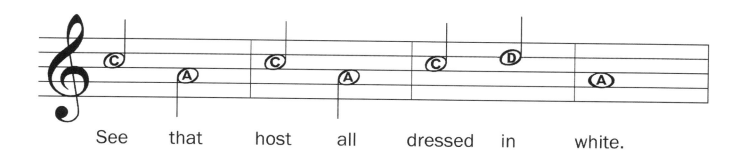

See that host all dressed in white.

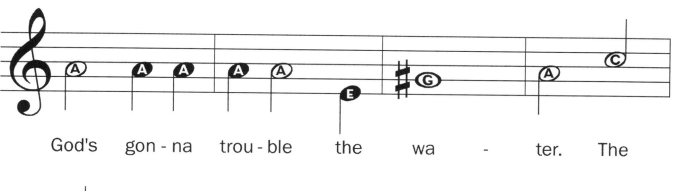

God's gon - na trou - ble the wa - ter. The

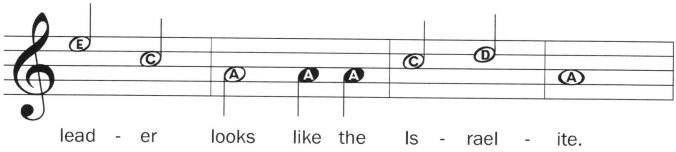

lead - er looks like the Is - rael - ite.

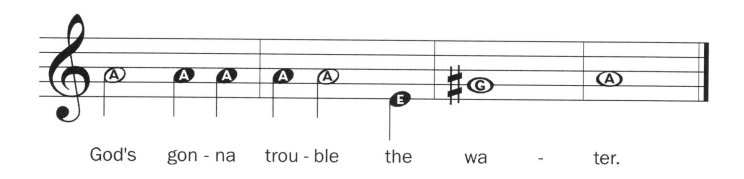

God's gon - na trou - ble the wa - ter.

Love Divine, All Loves Excelling

Charles Wesley and John Zundel

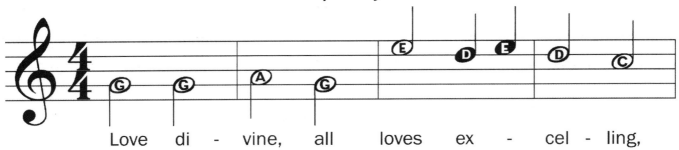

Love di - vine, all loves ex - cel - ling,

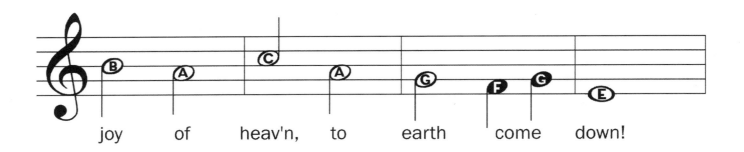

joy of heav'n, to earth come down!

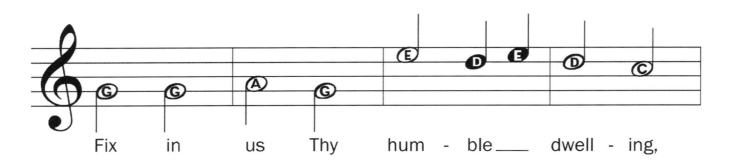

Fix in us Thy hum - ble___ dwell - ing,

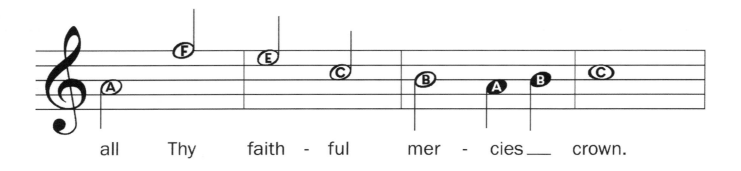

all Thy faith - ful mer - cies___ crown.

Love Divine, All Loves Excelling

Sweet Hour of Prayer

William Walford and William Bradbury

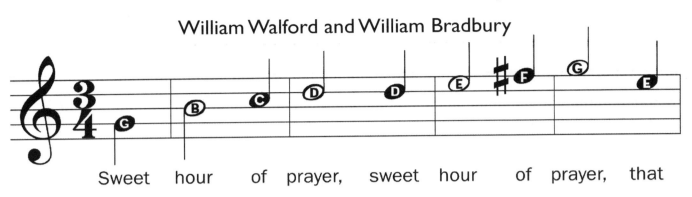

Sweet hour of prayer, sweet hour of prayer, that

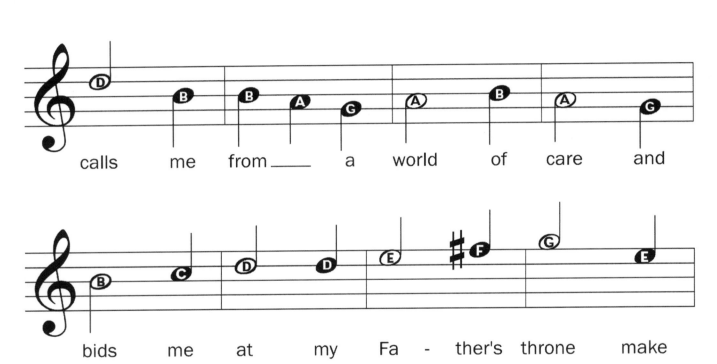

calls me from ____ a world of care and

bids me at my Fa - ther's throne make

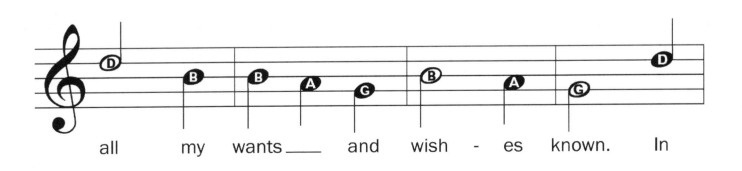

all my wants ____ and wish - es known. In

Sweet Hour of Prayer

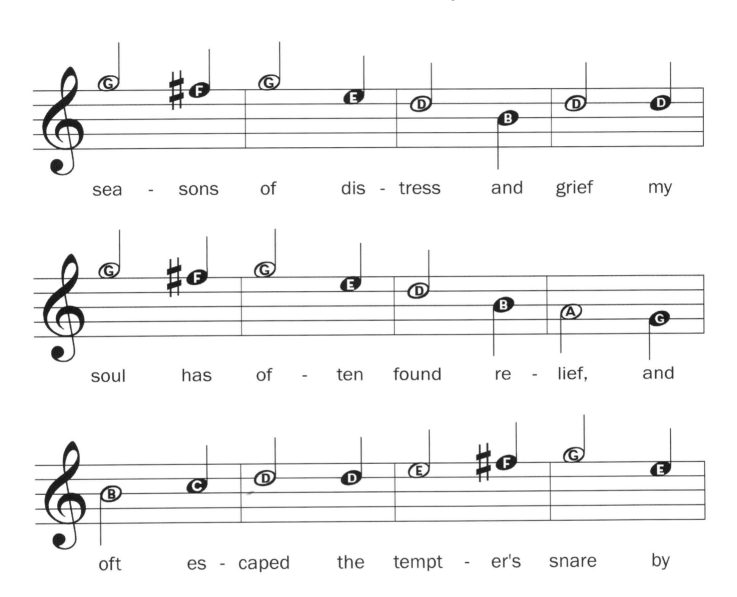

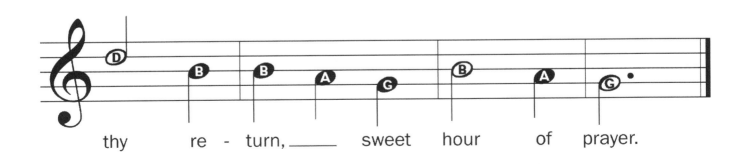

93

Rejoice, the Lord is King

Charles Wesley and John Darwall

Rejoice, the Lord is King

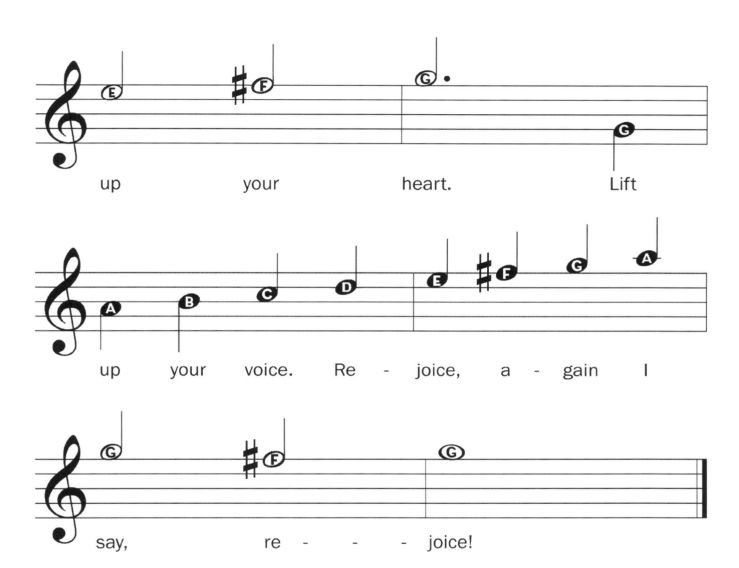

Soldiers of Christ, Arise

Charles Wesley and George J. Elvey

Soldiers of Christ, Arise

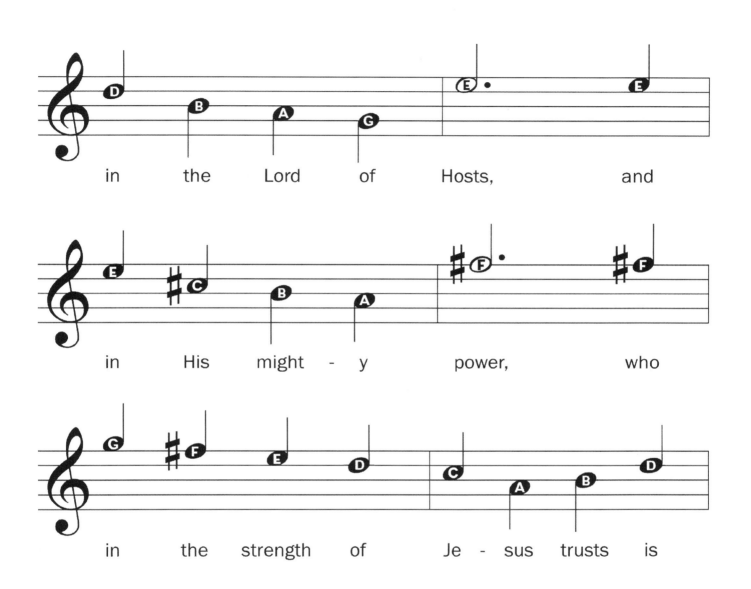

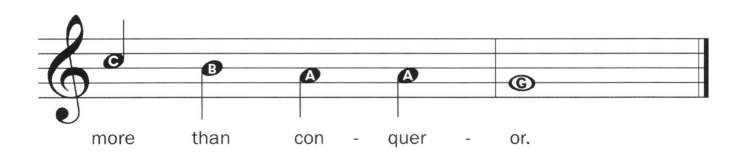

It Is Well

Horatio Gates Spafford and Philip Bliss

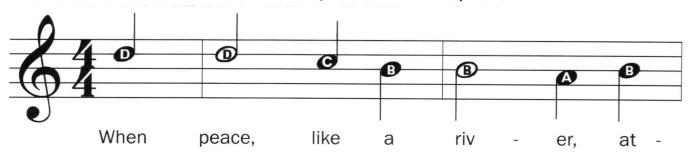

When   peace,   like   a   riv - er,   at -

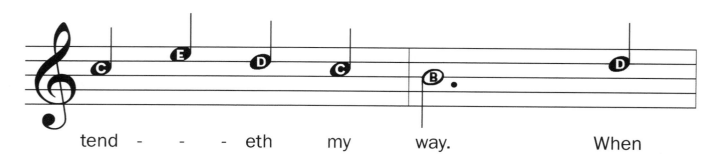

tend - - - eth   my   way.   When

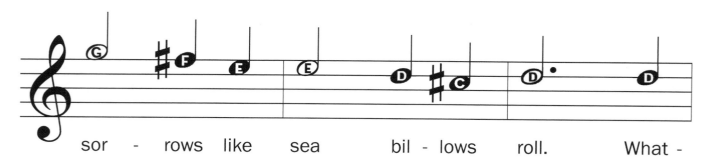

sor - rows   like   sea   bil - lows   roll.   What -

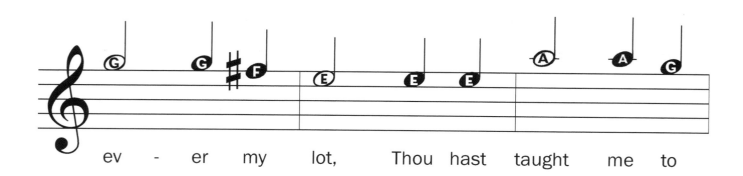

ev - er   my   lot,   Thou   hast   taught   me   to

It Is Well

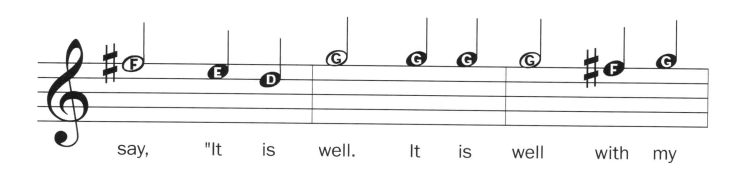

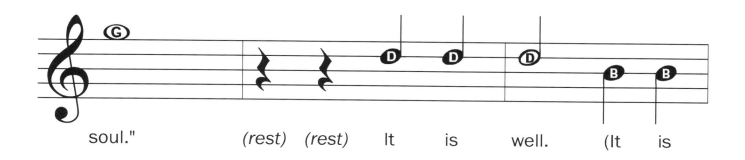

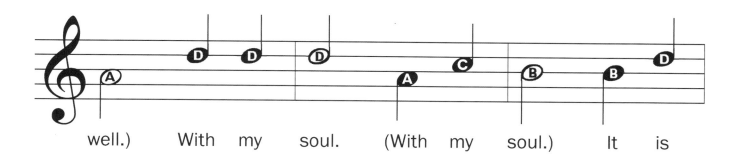

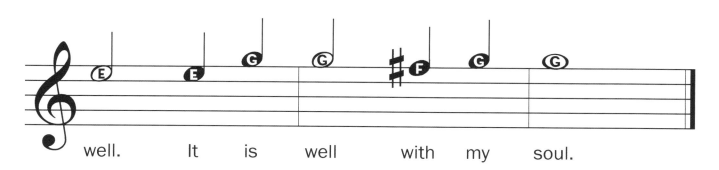

Blessed Assurance

Fanny J. Crosby and Phoebe Palmer Knapp

Bless-ed as - sur - ance, Je-sus is mine!

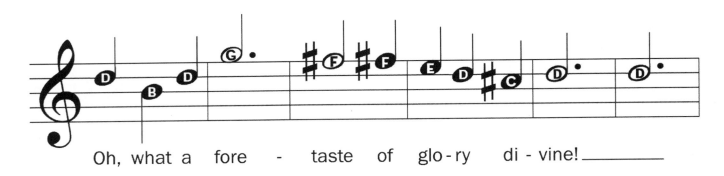

Oh, what a fore - taste of glo-ry di - vine!

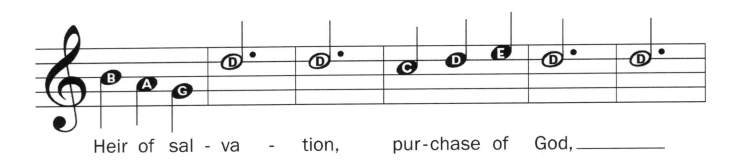

Heir of sal - va - tion, pur-chase of God,

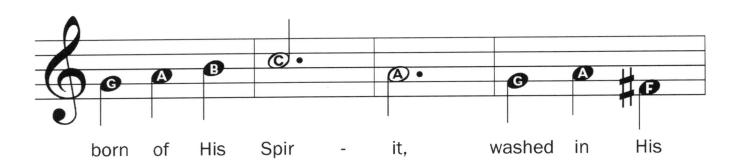

born of His Spir - it, washed in His

The Old Rugged Cross

George Bennard

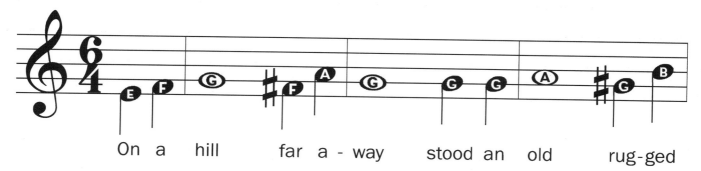

On a hill far a - way stood an old rug-ged

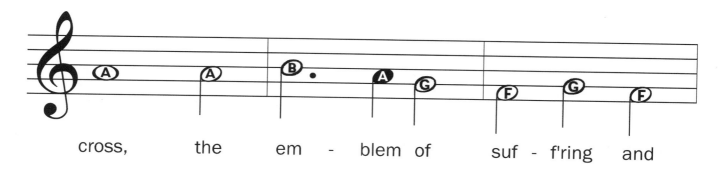

cross, the em - blem of suf - f'ring and

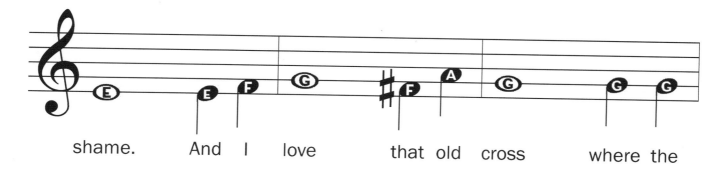

shame. And I love that old cross where the

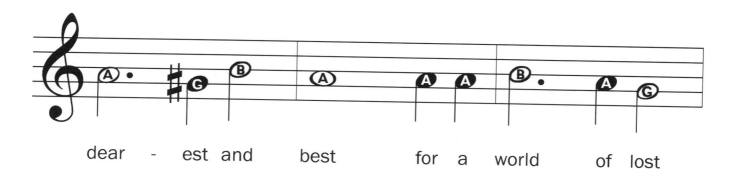

dear - est and best for a world of lost

The Old Rugged Cross

sin - ners was slain. So I'll cher - ish the old rug - ged

cross, till my tro - phies at last I lay

down. I will cling to the old rug - ged cross and ex-

change it some - day for a crown.

Bonus Downloads

This book includes free digital content.
Visit **www.avanellpublishing.com** or scan the QR code below
to access your bonus materials,

- Fully orchestrated recordings of each song

- Printable reference charts to use while you play

- Lessons and charts for left hand playing

- Practice tips to help you build your skills

- Sheet music of additional songs

Made in the USA
Columbia, SC
30 March 2025

55880203R00059